TOP 10 BUDAPEST

CONTENTS

4

Introducing Budapest

18

Top 10 Highlights

46

Top 10 of Everything

70

Area by Area

108

Streetsmart

INTRODUCING BUDAPEST

The lofty spire of Mátyás Church

WELCOME TO BUDAPEST

In Budapest, you can soak in thermal baths, admire Gothic and Art Nouveau architecture and cruise the mighty Danube – all in one unforgettable day. Don't want to miss a thing? With Top 10 Budapest, you'll enjoy the very best Hungary's capital has to offer.

As the Hungarian poet and revolutionary Sándor Petőfi once declared, "the Danube is the most beautiful river in the world when it flows through Budapest". It's hard to disagree with him. As the Danube swings through the centre of the Hungarian capital (dividing the now unified city into two historic entities, Buda and Pest), it flows past some of Budapest's most captivating buildings. There's the city's crown jewel, Buda Castle; the sprawling Parliament building, a frequent star on postcards; and a flurry of palatial buildings and grand bridges.

Views from Fisherman's Bastion

More incredible architecture awaits away from the river, too. Galleries in this city not only house masterpieces, but are themselves works of art: stand in awe of the epic Romanesque Hall in the Museum of Fine Arts or pause on the grand staircases of the Hungarian National Gallery. Places of worship are equally beautiful, too. In St Stephen's Basilica, gold-leaf dominates the decoration, while in the Great Synagogue, grand chandeliers hang from the ornately decorated ceiling. And then there are the baths. Built over springs first discovered by the Romans, the city's bath houses are beloved by locals for their healing waters and gorgeous architecture.

It's not all about the big attractions, however. Budapest's streets are wonderfully walkable. Wander down the cobblestone streets of the Castle District to find quiet, historic corners; stroll through Pest's leafy boulevards and you'll pass an array of tiny galleries; or spend a few hours in the Jewish Quarter and you might stumble across a dilapidated building, which just so happens to house a buzzy bar.

So, where to start? With Top 10 Budapest, of course. This pocket-sized guide gets to the heart of the city with simple lists of 10, expert local knowledge and comprehensive maps, helping you turn an ordinary trip into an extraordinary one.

THE STORY OF **BUDAPEST**

The modern city of Budapest has come a long way from its beginnings as a Roman frontier outpost. Through waves of conquest and revolution, the city has repeatedly risen from destruction to become the cultural heart of Hungary. Here's the story of how it came to be.

Budapest's Beginnings

The area now home to the Hungarian capital was first settled by Celtic peoples, who lived on the slopes of Gellért Hill. In the 1st century CE, they were conquered by the Romans, who swiftly established the town of Aquincum here. This urban centre served as the capital of a new Roman province (Lower Pannonia) and had all the markers of a sophisticated ancient settlement: amphitheatres, elaborate temple complexes and a host of thermal baths – the latter would become one of Budapest's defining characteristics. The settlement's strategic location at a dramatic bend in the powerful Danube river – a vital trade route connecting the Black Sea with Western Europe – made Aquincum one of the empire's most prosperous frontier cities.

After Rome's European decline, successive waves of tribal migrations swept through the Carpathian Basin. Little evidence remains of these rolling rulers of Aquincum; that is, until the Magyars arrived in 896 CE. These skilled horsemen from Central Asia brought a unique language and modern social structure to the town, establishing seven tribes throughout the region under Magyar leader, Árpád. His son, Stephen I, later took over and adopted Christianity for his people, becoming Hungary's first Christian king in 1000 CE. In the 12th century, the Árpáds (as the dynasty became known) also began to develop the areas of Buda and Pest. However, their future plans were shattered by the Mongol invasion of 1241–42, when ruler Batu Khan's forces destroyed the region. The Árpád dynasty had come to an end.

***The Siege of Buda in 1541* by Romeyn de Hooghe**

Medieval and Ottoman Rule

Recovery from the Mongol devastation was gradual but spectacular. In 1361, Buda officially became the royal capital of Hungary under the Austro-Hungarian Empire, replacing Székesfehérvár (the Árpáds' former capital) and marking its emergence as a major European power. The city's royal palace evolved into a magnificent complex, with merchants and artisans from across Europe establishing workshops beneath it.

This age of prosperity reached its zenith under King Mátyás Corvinus (1458–90), who transformed Buda into the most important centre of learning north of the Alps and oversaw a flourishing Renaissance court. The court's magnificence was legendary: tournaments, theatrical performances and scholarly debates drew Europe's elite to Hungary's capital.

Such splendour was cut short in 1541 when Suleiman the Magnificent's Ottoman forces conquered the city after a prolonged siege. The next 145 years of Turkish rule transformed the city's character. The Ottomans divided the city: Buda became a Turkish provincial seat, while Pest developed as a commercial centre. Mosques and minarets replaced churches, and Turkish baths joined Roman thermal springs.

The Mongol Invasion of Hungary in 1241

Moments in History

89 CE
Romans establish Aquincum on the Danube, founding the first major settlement on the site of modern Budapest.

896
Magyar tribes led by Árpád settle in the Carpathian Basin, establishing Christianity in the region and founding the Hungarian state.

1241
Mongol invasion devastates early Hungarian settlements, leaving the region in ruins for decades.

1361
Buda officially becomes the royal capital of Hungary, replacing Székesfehérvár as the seat of power.

1458
King Mátyás Corvinus begins his Renaissance reign, transforming Buda into a centre of learning and culture.

1686
Habsburg forces re-conquer Buda from the Ottomans after a brutal siege, ending Turkish occupation.

1848
Hungarian revolution erupts against Austrian rule, led by nationalist leaders such as Lajos Kossuth and Sándor Petőfi.

1918
The Austro-Hungarian Empire collapses, followed by a brief Hungarian Soviet Republic that lasts only 133 days.

1944
The siege of Budapest begins, becoming one of World War II's longest and bloodiest urban battles.

2004
Hungary joins the European Union, marking Budapest's full integration into the European community.

2023
Budapest hosts the World Athletics Championships.

Habsburg Era and Unification

The reconquest of Buda by Habsburg forces in 1686 marked the end of Ottoman rule, following a brutal siege led by Duke Charles of Lorraine. The city that emerged was dramatically different from the medieval Hungarian capital: a century of Islamic influence had left an indelible mark and the six-week long Habsburg siege had resulted in devastation. Under Habsburg rule, Buda and Pest began steady reconstruction. However, Hungarian aspirations for independence simmered beneath imperial control, ultimately erupting into the Hungarian Revolution of 1848–49, one of the most significant uprisings of the European Spring of Nations, a revolutionary wave that spread across Europe that year. Led by figures like Lajos Kossuth and Sándor Petőfi, revolutionaries demanded a constitutional government and national independence. Although initially successful, the revolution was ultimately crushed by Austrian and Russian forces.

One of the most transformative developments in the city's history came in 1873 with the unification of Buda, Pest and Óbuda (the city's north). This merger created modern Budapest and combined Buda's royal heritage with Pest's commercial energy. The unified city embarked on ambitious urban development, building the magnificent Parliament building and the continent's first underground railway.

The Habsburg empire re-capturing Buda

The Danube flowing past Budapest's Parliament building

Wars and Revolutions

The 20th century was a time of great change in Budapest. The collapse of the Austro-Hungarian Empire in 1918–1919 initially heralded independence for the country, but this was short-lived. Hungarian revolutionary Béla Kun overthrew Hungary's brief democratic government, ushering in an era of Communist rule under a new state: the Hungarian Soviet Republic. Lasting just 133 days, Kun's government was crushed by foreign intervention, and a period of political instability arrived.

Turmoil continued with World War II. The siege of Budapest from December 1944 to February 1945 was one of the war's longest urban battles, with German and Hungarian forces turning the city's streets into a battlefield against Soviet troops. All seven Danube bridges were systematically destroyed and the city's large Jewish population suffered horrific losses, with over 100,000 deported to death camps.

The post-war period saw Hungary ruled by the Soviet Union, but the country's independent spirit proved unbreakable. In 1956, student demonstrations erupted into a nationwide uprising against Soviet rule; workers joined students and revolutionary councils soon took control. For 13 days, Hungary seemed poised to break free from Soviet influence. However, massive Soviet military intervention crushed the revolution, killing over 2,500 Hungarians and forcing 200,000 to flee as refugees. Though defeated, the 1956 Revolution became a powerful symbol, inspiring democratic movements across Eastern Europe.

Budapest Today

Budapest's transformation began with communism's fall across Europe in 1989–90, when Hungary led Central and Eastern European nations towards democracy. The city re-emerged as a vibrant cultural and economic centre, attracting international investment while carefully restoring war-damaged monuments. In 2004, Hungary's entry into the European Union marked another milestone for European integration.

While Hungary has been ruled by Viktor Orbán's authoritarian national government since 2010, its capital has become an unexpected bastion of liberal values. The city has elected a string of liberal mayors and continues to support events such as Budapest Pride, despite national opposition.

TOP 10 EXPERIENCES

Planning the perfect trip to Budapest? Whether you're visiting for the first time or making a return trip, there are some things you simply shouldn't miss out on. To make the most of your time – and to enjoy the very best this wonderfully varied city has to offer – be sure to add these experiences to your list.

1 Soak in the baths

Budapest's thermal baths aren't just tourist attractions, they're an integral way of life in the city. Join locals playing chess in the warm mineral water of Széchenyi *(p97)* or luxuriate in the Ottoman-era Veli Bej Baths *(p55)*. It's relaxation with a distinctly Hungarian twist.

2 Cruise the Danube at twilight

Budapest is most beautiful when viewed from the water, and particularly at twilight. Hop on a river cruise as darkness falls and watch the Parliament building light up like something from a fairy tale. Many boats offer dinner and drinks onboard, too.

3 Explore Castle Hill

Lose yourself in the medieval cobblestoned streets of Castle Hill, where Hungarian kings walked centuries ago. Beyond the imposing Buda Castle *(p73)*, there are the turrets of Fisherman's Bastion, which offer jaw-dropping views across to Parliament *(p22)*.

4 Feast in historic markets

Hungry? Duck into markets like the Central Market Hall *(p62)* for a world of Hungarian flavours – picture mountains of red paprika, strings of spicy sausages and vendors hawking in quick-fire Hungarian. Local go-tos include crispy *lángos (p60)*, topped with sour cream, or sweet *kürtőskalács (p61)*.

5 Discover Budapest's 20th-century history

Budapest's modern history is memorialized across the city: stand before the cast-iron shoes on the Danube Bank *(p53)*, explore the chilling House of Terror *(p98)* or wander among Communist-era statues at Memento Park *(p104)*.

6 Hop on tram No 2

Hugging the scenic Danube embankment, this bright yellow tram offers million-dollar views of Parliament, Buda Castle and the Chain Bridge, all for the small price of a public transport ticket. Locals swear it's better than any tour bus.

7 Catch some music

In the mood for some classical music? Head to the acclaimed Liszt Academy of Music. Big-name pop acts more your thing? Book tickets to Sziget (one of Europe's largest music festivals). Whatever your taste, this city has music fans covered.

8 Experience café culture

Writers penning novels, revolutionaries plotting uprisings and lovers whispering sweet declarations: the city's coffee houses have seen it all. Seek out Café Gerbeaud *(p94)*, which has played host to 150 years of gossip, or the dazzlingly ornate New York Café *(p100)*.

9 Hike to epic viewpoints

Budapest rewards those willing to climb with breathtaking panoramas. Scale Gellért Hill *(p82)* as the sun sets over the Danube, turning the city golden, or escape to Normafa, where locals jog through beech forests just minutes from the downtown bustle.

10 Picnic on Margaret Island

Welcome to Budapest's green lung. A car-free oasis in the middle of the Danube, leafy Margaret Island *(p32)* offers a shady escape from the city. It's best explored by pedal car, available to rent around the island.

ITINERARIES

Strolling along the Danube river, unwinding in thermal baths, exploring a royal castle: there's a lot to see and do in Budapest. With places to eat, drink or simply take in the view, these itineraries offer ways to spend 2 days and 4 days in the city.

2 DAYS

Day 1

Morning

Begin your morning with a wander through Fisherman's Bastion *(p74)* for sunrise city views. The Neo-Gothic terraces offer an unparalleled view across the Danube to Parliament, giving you a great opportunity to get your bearings. The early morning light is magical here, plus you'll beat the crowds. Next, explore the colourful tiles and Gothic Revival architecture of Mátyás Church *(p38)*, a place quite literally fit for a king, as it was here that Hungarian monarchs were once crowned. Then wander the charming cobbled streets of Castle Hill, soaking up the medieval atmosphere before visiting the sprawling Buda Castle *(p73)*. Grab lunch at the Royal Guard Café, perfectly positioned for castle views.

SHOP

On Regi Posta utca, just off Váci utca, Bomo Art offers contemporary ceramics, textiles and jewellery made by local artists, all with a distinctly Hungarian flair.

Afternoon

Cross the iconic Chain Bridge *(p53)* into Pest – it was the first permanent bridge connecting Buda and Pest. Then take a moment to visit the Shoes on the Danube memorial *(p53)*, a moving commemoration of the victims of the Holocaust. Stroll along the Danube Promenade, taking in river views and historic architecture, before stopping off in Pest's legendary Gerbeaud café *(p94)*, where intellectuals have gathered since 1858, for coffee and pastries. For a spot of shopping and people watching, walk the full length of pedestrianized Váci utca *(p28)*. End your day with a sunset river cruise – Parliament illuminated from the water is an unforgettable sight.

Striking Gothic architecture of Mátyás Church

Day 2

Morning

Visit Parliament *(p22)* – booking in advance is essential for this Gothic Revival masterpiece that houses the Hungarian Crown Jewels – before exploring nearby Liberty Square (Szabadság tér; *p86*), home to monuments reflecting Hungary's complex revolutionary history. Then wander along the elegant Andrássy Avenue *(p96)*, a UNESCO World Heritage site lined with mansions and Neo-Renaissance buildings. Stop for a break at the Hungarian State Opera *(p40)*, where you can enjoy lunch in the opulent café as you admire the building's lavish interior.

Afternoon

Jump on the historic M1 metro line (continental Europe's first underground railway) from Opera to Heroes' Square *(p98)*. This grand spot celebrates Hungary's millennium with its impressive central colonnade. Now it's the time to relax: make your way to Széchenyi Baths *(p97)*, Europe's largest medicinal baths, and take some time out to unwind in both the indoor and outdoor thermal pools. See out the day with dinner and drinks at Gundel *(p101)* in City Park, a legendary restaurant that's been serving refined Hungarian cuisine since 1894.

The central colonnade in Heroes' Square

VIEW
Taking a walk along the Chain Bridge provides stunning views back towards Buda Castle, giving you the chance to capture unobstructed shots of one of Budapest's defining landmarks.

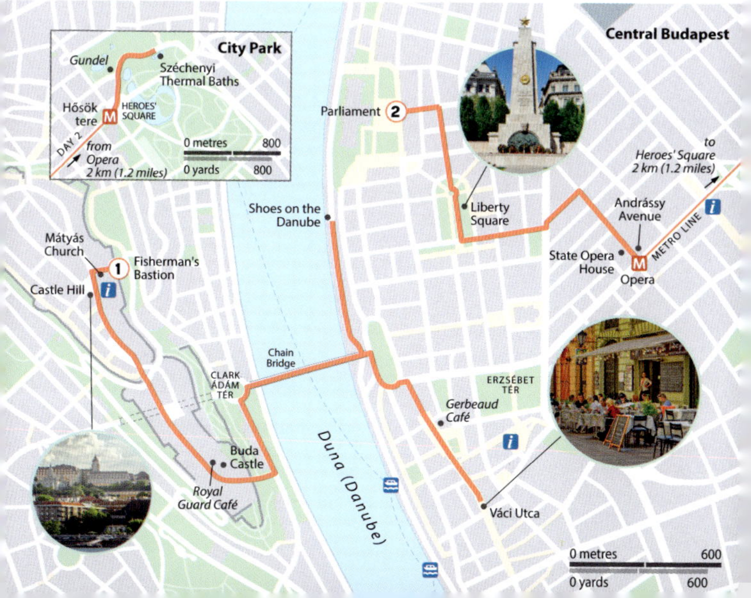

Central Budapest
City Park
Gundel
Széchenyi Thermal Baths
Hősök tere
HEROES' SQUARE
DAY 2
from Opera 2 km (1.2 miles)
0 metres 800
0 yards 800
Parliament
Shoes on the Danube
Liberty Square
to Heroes' Square 2 km (1.2 miles)
Andrássy Avenue
METRO LINE
State Opera House
Opera
Mátyás Church
Fisherman's Bastion
Castle Hill
Chain Bridge
CLARK ÁDÁM TÉR
ERZSÉBET TÉR
Gerbeaud Café
Buda Castle
Royal Guard Café
Duna (Danube)
Váci Utca
0 metres 600
0 yards 600

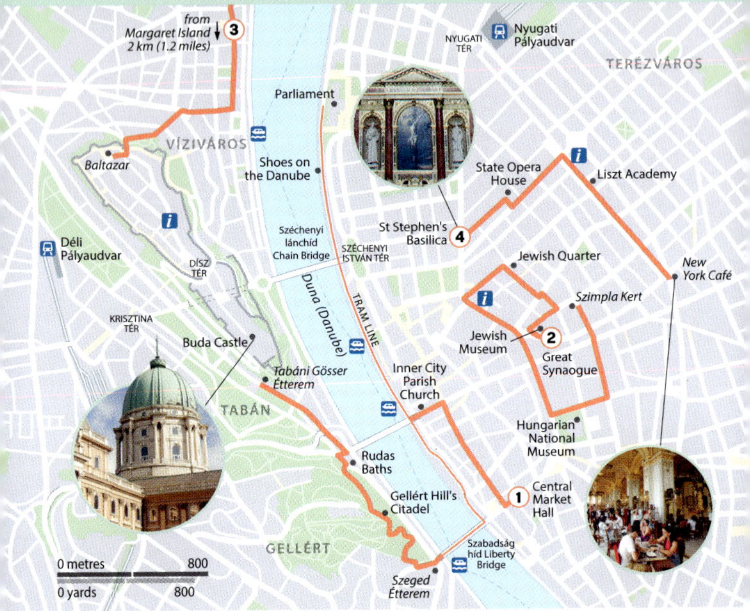

4 DAYS

Day 1

Start the day at Central Market Hall *(p62)*, a magnificent 19th-century market where locals shop for paprika, fresh produce and traditional treats. Food stalls upstairs are a great choice for breakfast – look out for *lángos (p60)*. Next, visit nearby Inner City Parish Church *(p91)*, Budapest's oldest church, which survived Ottoman occupation and heavy World War II bombing. Take the scenic Tram No 2 along the Danube Embankment to view the Shoes on the Danube *(p53)* in memory of the city's thousands of Holocaust victims. From there, it's just a short walk to the Hungarian Parliament *(p22)*. For lunch, cross to Buda to sample Hungarian cuisine at Szeged Étterem *(p83)*, before spending a relaxing afternoon at the Rudas Baths *(p54)* – among the oldest in the city and full of Ottoman-era opulence. Catch sunset from Gellért Hill's Citadel *(p80)* for panoramic city views. Enjoy dinner the in the lively Tabán district – Restaurant Tabáni Gösser Étterem *(Attila út 19)* is a great bet for traditional Hungarian dishes.

Fresh produce for sale at Central Market Hall

TRANSPORT
Take the impressive M1 metro line from Opera to Oktogon. As continental Europe's first underground railway, it is beautifully preserved with original details and vintage carriages from 1896.

Day 2

Begin your second day in the city by exploring the Great Synaogue *(p44)* and Jewish Museum. It is Europe's largest synagogue and tells the story of Hungarian Jewish life through centuries of triumph and tragedy. Next, discover the vibrant Jewish Quarter's street art and boutiques, where "ruin bars" sit alongside independent design shops. Browse for local Hungarian crafts and souvenirs such as contemporary ceramics, textiles and jewellery. Pause for lunch at a trendy café in the quarter, such as Blue Bird Cafe, then visit the Hungarian National Museum *(p42)* to understand the nation's complex history through its many artifacts and exhibitions. Finish your day with dinner and drinks at legendary bar Szimpla Kert *(p94)*, the original "ruin pub" that sparked Budapest's alternative nightlife scene.

Day 3

Spend the morning exploring the car-free zone of Margaret Island *(p32)*, either by bike or on foot – this green oasis in the Danube offers gardens, ruins and a plethora of recreational facilities. Visit the UNESCO-listed Water Tower and listen to the musical Bodor Well, a perfect pre-lunch activity. Enjoy a relaxing picnic lunch on the island before walking off your meal with a climb up the restored Elizabeth Lookout Tower for spectacular views across the city and Danube bend. Return to the city for dinner in the Castle District at Baltazár *(p77)*, which is known for its excellent steaks and wine.

Spectators taking in the musical fountain on Margaret Island

Day 4

For your final day, start with a visit to Hungary's largest church, St Stephen's Basilica *(p26)*, and climb the dome for 360-degree views of the city. The basilica houses the mummified hand of the nation's first king, which makes for a grisly but fascinating sight. Next, explore the impressive Hungarian State Opera *(p40)* and enjoy a coffee and a light lunch in its lavish café, admiring the former workplace of renowned composer Gustav Mahler. Just a short walk away, visit Liszt Academy *(p37)* for more classical music heritage – this Art Nouveau masterpiece still hosts world-class concerts, as it has done for centuries. Make a stop to revel in Budapest's café culture at the stunning New York Café *(p100)*, considered one of the world's most beautiful spots for a caffeine fix, where you can also enjoy dinner and a cocktail to toast the end of your trip. End the evening with a classical concert or opera performance.

TOP 10 HIGHLIGHTS

Interior of St Stephen's Basilica

EXPLORE THE HIGHLIGHTS

There are some sights in Budapest you simply shouldn't miss, and it's these attractions that make the Top 10. Discover what makes each one a must-see on the following pages.

VÁCI ÚT
DÓZSA GYÖRGY ÚT
LEHEL UTCA
VÁGÁNY UTCA
DÓZSA GYÖRGY ÚT
DÓZSA GYÖRGY ÚT
4
PODMANICZKY UTCA
IZABELLA UTCA
TERÉZVÁROS
DAMJANICH UTCA
DEMBINSZKY UTCA
8
ANDRÁSSY ÚT
CSÁNYI U
KIRÁLY U
WESSELÉNYI U
KLAUZÁL U
10
RÁKÓCZI ÚT
KOSSUTH L. U
MÚZEUM KRT
JÓZSEFVÁROS
SZENTKIRÁLYI U
9
1 Parliament
2 St Stephen's Basilica
3 Váci Street
4 Hungarian House of Music
5 Margaret Island
6 Hungarian National Gallery
7 Mátyás Church
8 Hungarian State Opera
9 Hungarian National Museum
10 Great Synagogue

PARLIAMENT

J1 V, Kossuth Lajos tér 1–3 8am–4pm daily (Apr–Oct: to 6pm)
parlament.hu

In 1846, the Hungarian poet Mihály Vörösmarty famously lamented "the motherland has no home". Decades later, in 1902, when Hungary opened its Parliament building, it not only had a home, but one that could claim to be one of the finest Neo-Gothic buildings in Europe. Designed by Imre Steindl, it's one of Budapest's defining landmarks.

1 Cross-Danube Vista

Sensational close up, the Hungarian Parliament is arguably even better from afar. The building is scenically set along the banks of the Danube, and its iconic façade is lit up at night.

2 Main Entrance

Inspired by London's Houses of Parliament, and built with no expense spared, the main entrance is guarded by two lions sculpted by Hungarian artists Béla Markup and József Somogyi.

3 Grand Staircase

The sumptuous main staircase is decorated with three outstanding ceiling frescoes. These include Károly Lotz's *Glorification of Hungary*, depicting scenes from the lives of the country's kings and saints.

TOP TIP

You can explore the sight only through a guided tour when Parliament is not in session.

4 Delegation Room

This room was the meeting place for parliamentarians and ministry delegates. The elaborate artworks adorning its walls are by Hungarian painter Andor Dudits, and the ceiling paintings, *Wisdom* and *Fortitude*, are by famous 19th-century painter Károly Lotz.

5 National Assembly Hall

The Hungarian Lower House is where Parliament sits. The bullet hole above the lectern dates

Clockwise from right **Lion statue guarding the main entrance; St Stephen's Holy Crown and Royal Sword in the Domed Hall; grand main staircase; former Hungarian Upper House**

The Neo-Gothic Hungarian Parliament, beside the Danube

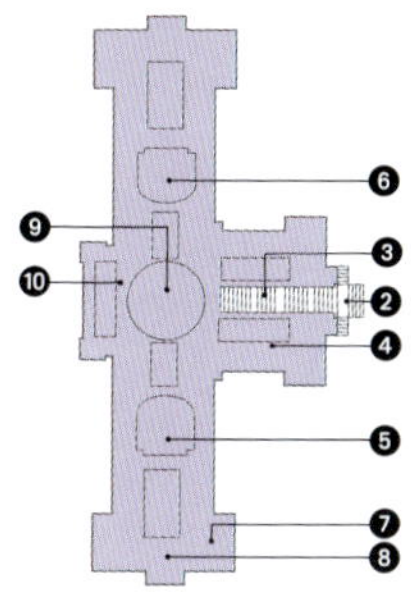

Parliament Site Plan

from 1912, when an assassin tried to kill the speaker, István Tisza.

6 Congress Hall

In 1944, Hungary became a unicameral state with a single legislative chamber. Since then, the former Upper House has not been used for legislation, but it still features a rich interior with a painting by Hungarian artist Zsigmond Vajda of the monk Astrik handing St Stephen his crown.

7 Prime Minister's Office

The prime minister's office is closed to visitors, but you can admire its reception rooms, with paintings by Géza Udvary and Antal Diósy.

8 The Conquest

Hungarian Realist painter Mihály Munkácsy's artwork, *The Conquest*, was originally created for the Chamber of Commons, but was rejected as it was deemed a misrepresentation of the first contact between the invading Magyars and Pannonian tribes as a peaceful meeting rather than a conquest.

9 Crown Jewels

Spirited out of the country after World War II – and kept in Fort Knox, USA, until 1978 – the Holy Crown and the Royal Sceptre are now housed in the Domed Hall.

10 Domed Hall

The spiritual heart of the building, the Domed Hall was once used to host joint sessions of Parliament. Each of the 16 pillars supporting the dome features a statue of a Hungarian king or queen *(p24)*. The hall is now used for official ceremonies.

IMRE STEINDL

Before submitting his entry for the contest to design Hungary's Parliament, Hungarian architect Imre Steindl had proposed designs for a parliament in Berlin, which were rejected. Berlin's loss was Hungary's gain as Steindl's vision resulted in a masterpiece. He is remembered with a bust on the main staircase.

Domed Hall Statues

1. Prince Árpád
Prince Árpád was the leader of the Magyar tribes – who migrated from the Ural mountains in present-day Russia and settled on the Pannonian plains in 896 CE. His son was Stephen I.

2. St Stephen
St Stephen (István I) was elected Duke of the Magyars in 997 CE. He adopted Christianity soon after, and was crowned king by Pope Sylvester II in 1001.

3. St Ladislaus
Hungary's ruler from 1077 to 1095, Ladislaus (László I) was victorious against the Turks and the Cumans, and annexed Croatia in 1092.

4. András II
The son of King Béla III, András II was crowned in 1205. He expanded the Magyar state, conquering swathes of Transylvania and encouraging vast numbers of Magyars to settle in the region.

5. Béla IV
Defeated by the Tatars in 1241, Béla IV survived to rebuild Hungary after the Tatars left the country in ashes a year later. His patient rebuilding of the nation over the next 25 years elevated him to greatness.

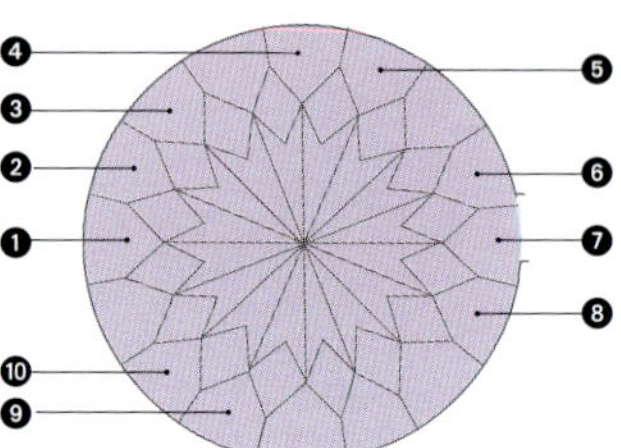

Layout of Domed Hall Statues

6. Louis I
Crowned in 1342, Louis (Lajos) the Great reigned for 40 years. In 1370, he formed a political union with Poland after the death of his uncle, the Polish king Casimir III, and ruled as sovereign of both until his death in 1382.

7. János Hunyadi
A gifted commander, Hunyadi became the ruler of Transylvania in 1441 and then Governor of Hungary in 1446. He is remembered for defeating the Turks in the Battle of Belgrade in 1456.

8. Mátyás Corvinus
In 1458, at the age of 15, Mátyás was crowned king and went on to become Hungary's greatest monarch. A Renaissance man, he valued the sciences, arts and architecture.

9. Charles III
In 1687, Hungary renounced its right to elect its own king. Thereupon, Charles VI, the last Holy Roman Emperor of the Habsburg dynasty, inherited the throne and became Charles VI King of Bohemia and Charles III King of Hungary.

10. Maria Theresa
Maria Theresa acceded to the throne in 1740, ruling Hungary until 1780. During her reign, Buda became an imperial city, thriving as a centre of central European art, second only to Vienna.

Sculpture of Prince Árpád flanked by statues

THE DOMED HALL

The first section of Parliament to be completed was the Domed Hall in 1896. Designed to convey a sense of amplified space, the 16-sided dome, with its ceiling covered in Neo-Gothic gilding, is 96 m (315 ft) high – a feat it shares with the dome of St Stephen's Basilica *(p26)*, signifying that the Church and State have equal footing in Hungary. The number 96 also has symbolic value in the country, as it was in 896 CE that Hungarian Magyars first arrived in the region, leading to the country's development as a political entity. Each of the 16 pillars supporting the dome bears the statue and coat of arms of a significant Hungarian ruler. Apart from the ten dignitaries mentioned overleaf *(p24)*, the six remaining statues represent key figures in Hungarian history (in clockwise direction): Könyves Kálmán, András III, István Báthory, István Bocskai, Gábor Bethlen and Leopold II. The Domed Hall also served as the venue for a special session of Parliament held during Budapest's Millennium Celebrations.

TOP 10
DATES IN THE PARLIAMENT'S HISTORY

1. 12 Oct 1885: Foundation stone is laid.
2. 15 Mar 1896: First session of Parliament is held.
3. 1902: Parliament building is completed.
4. 4 Jun 1912: An assassin attempts to shoot the Speaker.
5. 4 Jun 1920: Treaty of Trianon is signed, stripping Hungary of two-thirds of its territory.
6. 1944: Hungary becomes a unicameral republic with a single legislative body.
7. 23 Oct 1956: Armed uprising against Soviet rule – tanks intervene, a new government is set up.
8. 16 Jun 1958: Execution of popular Prime Minister Imre Nagy *(p104)*.
9. 23 Oct 1989: Hungary is proclaimed a republic and multi-party elections are allowed by Communists.
10. 2 May 1990: MPs take their seats after post-Communist elections.

The Parliament's impressive gilded dome rising over a sixteen-sided central hall

2

ST STEPHEN'S BASILICA

L2 Szent István tér Basilica: 9am–5:15pm daily (from 12:30pm Sun); Dome and Treasury: 9am–6:30pm daily bazilikabudapest.hu

Splendidly lit in the evening, this beautifully sprawling basilica, with its 96-m (315-ft) dome, is visible from all over Budapest and is perhaps the most-photographed sight in the city. Built between 1851 and 1905 to mark the 1000th anniversary of the Magyars in Hungary, its layout takes the form of a Greek cross.

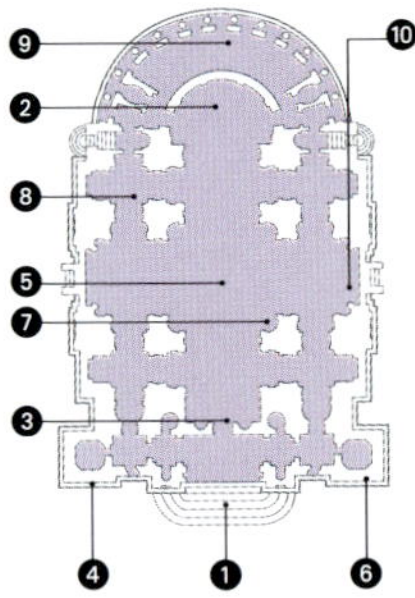

St Stephen's Basilica Site Plan

1 Main Entrance

"I am the way and the truth and the life" proclaims the Latin inscription above the basilica's main entrance. Situated above the inscription are several statues of Hungarian saints paying homage to the Virgin Mary and the infant Jesus.

2 Main Altar

A life-size marble statue of St Stephen (King István), the first Hungarian Christian king, by sculptor Alajos Stróbl, dominates the main altar of the basilica. On either side, fine paintings by the 19th-century artist Gyula Benczúr depict scenes from the saint-king's life.

3 Main Portal

The oak front door is decorated with medallions that depict the heads of the 12 Apostles. Despite the door's age, the carvings remain an impressive sight.

4 North Tower

The 9,144-kg (9-ton) bell in the North Tower was paid for by German

Sumptuous interior of the basilica

TOP TIP

On St Stephen's Day, you can see the Holy Right Hand being carried outside by the priests.

Catholics, who were ashamed that the Nazis had looted the original at the end of World War II during their retreat from Budapest. The original bell was never traced.

5 Dome and Mosaics

The Neo-Renaissance dome, designed by Miklós Ybl in 1867, replaced the original dome by József Hild, which collapsed due to poor workmanship and materials. Visitors can reach the dome by climbing 302 steps, or by taking the lift and then walking up 42 steps. Inside, the dome is adorned with mosaics by Károly Lotz. Above the cupola, a viewing platform offers superb views of the city; it is reached by a lift and stairs.

6 Treasury

A replica of the holy Hungarian crown forms the centrepiece of a small collection of religious jewellery. The original crown of St Stephen is now kept in the Domed Hall of the Hungarian Parliament *(p23)*. Gifts to Hungarian kings from a succession of popes are also on display here.

7 St Gellért and St Emeric

Alajos Stróbl carved the statue of St Gellért and his pupil, St Emeric (St Stephen's son, Imre), that stands in a small nave in the centre of the main hall. Opposite is a statue of St Elizabeth by Károly Senyei.

8 Holy Right Hand

The mummified forearm of St Stephen is displayed in the Holy Right Hand Chapel near the main altar. It was taken to Croatia by Béla IV in the 13th century to protect it from the Tatars. After time in Vienna and at the Royal Palace in Buda, it was brought back here on 20 August 1945 (St Stephen's Day).

ORGAN CONCERTS

The basilica's organ was made by Angster & Sons of Pécs, and installed in 1904. At the time, it was considered the world's finest organ. It was enlarged in 1934, and today comprises no fewer than 5,898 pipes. You can hear it at special organ concerts, which are held in the basilica from time to time.

9 Figures of the 12 Apostles

The rear colonnade of the basilica has 12 superb statues by Leó Feszler representing the 12 Apostles. Below is a fine Neo-Classical loggia.

10 Gyula Benczúr Painting

The painting *St Stephen*, by Gyula Benczúr, portrays the king – who died without an heir – proffering the care of the country and the crown to the Virgin Mary.

Sacred Holy Right Hand relic

3

VÁCI STREET

C4–C5

Home to many grand buildings dating back to the 19th century, Váci utca (Váci Street) is one of the city's most popular streets. With two parts – the northern end for shopping and the southern end for drinking and eating – it buzzes with life day and night, and serves as the city's commercial and social hub. Most of the street is pedestrianized, apart from where it is bisected by the access road to Elizabeth Bridge.

1 Gerbeaud Cukrászda

Since 1858, Gerbeaud Cukrászda *(p94)* has been known for its richly decorated interior, its aromatic coffee and the mouth-watering Dobos torte (a famous Hungarian sponge cake, p60).

2 1000 Tea

Váci Street has lots of places to eat, drink and while away the hours, but a relaxing oasis away from the hustle and bustle is 1000 Tea *(p94)*. This quiet café has a selection of loose-leaf teas from all over the world.

Philanthia, Budapest's most popular florist

3 Central Market Hall

Built in 1897 in Neo-Gothic style, Budapest's largest market *(p62)* is well worth a visit. It has a number of stalls selling local handicrafts as well as vegetables, fish and cheese. Specialities include spicy *kolbász* salami and sheep's cheese.

4 Thonet House

V, Váci utca 11

Built between 1888 and 1890 by famed Secessionist architects Ödön Lechner and Gyula Pártos, Thonet House is most notable for the beautiful Zsolnay tiles that adorn its façade.

5 Philanthia

V, Váci utca 9
10:30am–6pm Mon–Sat

Opened in 1905, this Secession-style florist now occupies part of the Neo-Classical block at No 9. The block was built in 1840 by József Hild and was once occupied by the Inn of the Seven Electors, which had a large ball-room where the well-known composer Franz Liszt performed when he was just 12 years old.

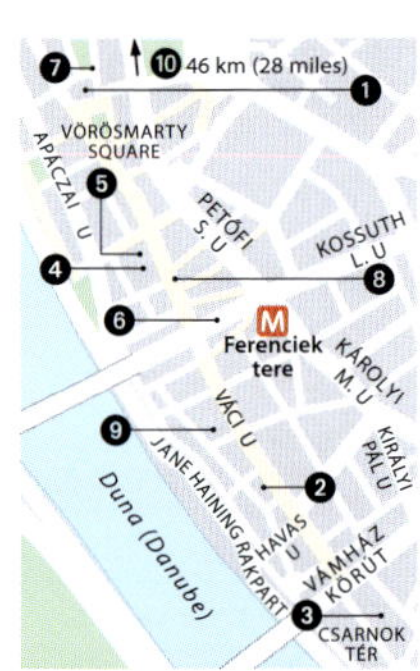

6 St Michael's City Church

Váci utca 47/b
Hours vary, check website **szentmihalytemplom.hu**

First built around 1230, St Michael's City Church was devastated by the Turks in 1541, rebuilt in 1701 and then renovated between 1964 and 1968. Its plain exterior belies a rich interior, including a gold pulpit and dome.

EAT

At Krumplis Lángos *(Váci utca 76)* you can sample heavenly *lángos*, a fried flatbread, often made with potatoes, perfect for eating as you stroll.

Vintage train, Vörösmarty Square Metro Station

7 Vörösmarty Square Metro Station

This metro station is one of the prettiest in Budapest. It's decorated with elegant tiles and dotted with wooden booths; the tiny yellow trains running through it are enchanting, too.

8 Klotild Palaces

Váci utca 34

Forming a splendid entrance to Elizabeth Bridge *(p52)*, the twin Klotild Palaces were commissioned by Archduchess Klotild, daughter-in-law of Emperor Franz József, and finished in 1902. While their interiors mostly house shops or offices, the southern palace, Matild Palace, is home to a luxury hotel.

9 The Promenade

Walking the full length of Váci Street from Vörösmarty Square to Vámház körút is a must-do experience. Along the way, take in the atmosphere, the bustle and the stunning architecture. Note that it can get very crowded in summer.

WHAT'S IN A NAME?

The name of Budapest's famous street has simple origins. The street was once the main road linking Pest to the town of Vác *(p69)*. The gate leading to Vác used to stand at Váci utca No 3.

10 Palais Herend

Located in József Nádor tér, Palais Herend *(p62)* is the largest of Budapest's porcelain shops. It is one of the few spots in the city to sell genuine Herend ceramics, famous for their intricacy and quality. It also screens short films showing how porcelain is made.

Exploring the busy Váci Street

HUNGARIAN HOUSE OF MUSIC

F2 Olof Palme sétány 3–5 10am–6pm Tue–Sun (to 8pm Thu)
zenehaza.hu

Opened in 2021 as the crown jewel of the ambitious Liget Project to rejuvenate City Park, the House of Music brings together Hungary's musical heritage with its contemporary ambitions. Masterfully designed by Japanese architect Sou Fujimoto, this eye-catching building is both a museum and a popular concert venue.

1 Façade

The striking glass-curtain exterior combines modern architectural techniques with traditional materials to create a spectacular building that has won several awards. Fujimoto's vision was to close the gap between the natural world and modern environments, giving visitors the feeling that they're still strolling around City Park even after they've stepped inside the building.

2 Roof

Designed to resemble a honeycomb, the building's undulating roof is a series of concentric circles that radiate from the centre, mimicking soundwaves passing through the air. The crater-like holes on it allow light to cascade into the building.

3 Dimensions of Sound

The museum's permanent exhibition, Dimensions of Sound, offers a hands-on, interactive journey through the history of music. A treat for the eyes and ears, it features the work of both Hungarian and international composers, musicians and pop and rock stars.

4 Creative Sound Space

Eight installations that are a part of the main exhibition allow visitors to create their own music by combining a variety of pre-recorded sounds

Ceiling representing a forest canopy

from a multitude of instruments. Visual effects complement the music.

5 Concert Hall

The concert hall, which can seat 320 or accommodate 500 people standing, hosts concerts most days and evenings. The acoustics are stunning, regardless of whether classical, folk, electronic, or rock music is being performed.

6 Sound Dome

In the underground level lies a unique 360-degree dome that combines a projection screen with a state-of-the-art sound system to immerse visitors in the world of music. The first show plays sounds and images from the Carpathian Basin, creating an incredible acoustic and visual experience.

7 Music Garden

A café and terrace in the landscaped garden allow visitors to fully appreciate the remarkable design of the House of Music as they sip on coffee, wine, or cocktails. There's also a music-themed playground for children.

8 Open-air Concerts

On most afternoons and evenings during spring and summer, concerts by up-and-coming bands from a variety of musical backgrounds are held in the small amphitheatre.

9 Bistro

Noon–8pm Tue–Sat

The bistro serves a good selection of Hungarian food and wine. At lunchtime, students from the Budapest Academy of Music often provide musical accompaniment.

10 Piano Nights

Every Thursday evening, the bistro hosts piano concerts featuring jazz and popular movie scores performed by talented local pianists.

Unique honeycomb roof structure

THE LIGET PROJECT

Intended to transform City Park in much the same way as the Millennium Exhibition of 1896 *(p98)*, Liget is an ongoing project of cultural renewal that, besides the House of Music, also includes the Ethnographic Museum *(p99)*, a planned new Hungarian House of Innovation and a National Gallery. When complete, this ambitious cultural quarter will consolidate Budapest's position as a major European cultural destination, creating a unified museum district to rival Vienna's MuseumsQuartier.

5

MARGARET ISLAND

B1

Inhabited since Roman times, Margaret Island (Margitsziget), a green oasis in the middle of the Danube, has served as Budapest's playground since 1869. It is named after Princess Margit, daughter of King Béla IV, who spent most of her life in the island's convent in the 13th century. The island was also once a popular hunting ground for medieval kings.

1 Centenary Monument

The striking Modernist Centenary Monument was installed in 1973 to commemorate the unification of Buda, Óbuda and Pest to form Budapest in 1873.

2 Water Tower

Built in 1911, the UNESCO-protected Water Tower stands 57 m (187 ft) tall. Its viewing gallery at the top offers lovely panoramic views of the island. During the summer season, the tower also serves as an exhibition hall.

3 Dominican Convent

One of the island's most important monuments is the ruin of a 13th-century Dominican convent. It was founded by King Béla IV, whose daughter Margit came to live here in 1251. A plaque in the church marks the spot where she is buried.

4 Franciscan Church

The secluded ruins of the 14th-century Franciscan Church lie in the island's centre. Though there is very little left to admire of the once-spectacular Gothic structure, it still has a fine arched window and a staircase.

TOP TIP

In summer, public boats marked D12 run on the Danube, stopping twice at the island.

5 St Michael's Church

The oldest building on Margaret Island, St Michael's Church was founded in the 11th century, but it was devastated by the Turks in 1541. What visitors see today is a 1930s reconstruction, which used materials salvaged from the original building.

Bronze statue in the Japanese Garden

6 Japanese Garden

There are three lovely landscaped gardens on the island, but the most delightful is the Japanese Garden at its northern end. This tranquil space is home to a wide variety of tropical plants, lily pools and waterfalls.

7 Musical Fountain

From March to October, this fountain leaps into action morning and night, shooting water in time to a classical piece or a pop song. Coloured lights are added for evening performances.

8 Bodor Well

A replica of a long-destroyed 1820 well from Târgu Mures in Romania, the unusual musical Bodor Well dates from 1936 and plays recorded music on the hour.

9 Palatinus Strand

Opened in 1919, the city's largest outdoor pool complex buzzes from dawn to dusk, as people relax in the therapeutic waters pumped from the island's thermal springs *(p55)*. There are water slides and special pools for children, too.

Distinctive Water Tower amid lush greenery

10 Ensana Thermal Margaret Island

This legendary hotel designed by Miklós Ybl opened in 1872. For years, it was the most fashionable in the city, attracting aristocracy from all over Europe. Today, it has been joined by a sister spa *(p55)*.

PRINCESS MARGIT (MARGARET)

After the horrors of the Mongol invasion in 1241–42, a desperate King Béla IV offered to give his daughter to God if, in return, he would keep the Mongols away. In 1251, Béla sent the nine-year-old Princess Margit to the island's convent, where she stayed for the rest of her life. The Mongols never returned.

HUNGARIAN NATIONAL GALLERY

H4 Royal Palace buildings A, B, C and D 10am–6pm Tue–Sun mng.hu

The treasure trove that is the Hungarian National Gallery has been housed in the Royal Palace since 1975. It displays pieces from medieval times to the present day with a particular focus on Secessionist art. The gallery has six permanent exhibitions presenting the finest pieces from its collection, which it shares with the Museum of Fine Arts.

1 Main Entrance

Part of the 18th-century Maria Theresa Palace, the late Baroque façade exhibits an eclectic range of influences.

2 Habsburg Crypt

This crypt, with the exquisite sarcophagus of Palatine Archduke Joseph, is a Neo-Classical warren of black-and-white marble and gold leaf. It can only be seen on a guided tour.

3 Great Throne Room

An entire room of the gallery is devoted to 15th- and 16th-century Gothic altarpieces. The best, painted in 1520 at a church in Kisszeben (Sabinov, in present-day Slovakia), depicts St Anne and St John the Baptist.

Hungarian National Gallery Floorplan

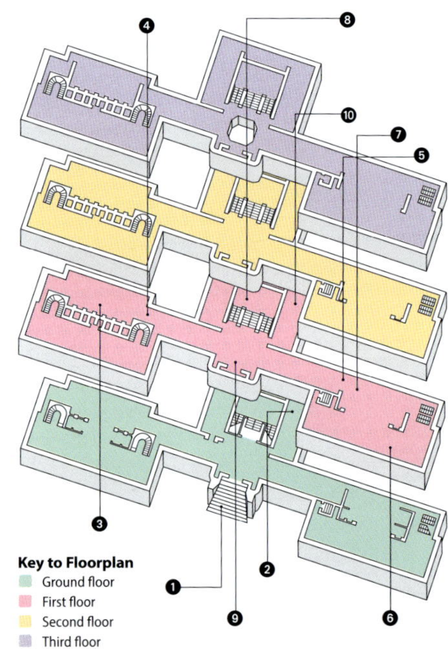

TOP TIP

The gallery can be visited for free on 15 Mar, 20 Aug and 23 Oct (national holidays).

4 The Visitation

Nothing is known about Master MS, who was the chief exponent of late Gothic painting in Hungary. His best work (*The Visitation*; 1500–10), depicts the Virgin Mary meeting St Elizabeth.

5 Women of Eger

Besides his fine portrait work, Hungarian painter Bertalan Székely created a number of historical works featuring simple, heroic female figures in a Romantic style. *Women of Eger* (1867)

Admiring the gallery's extensive collection

GALLERY GUIDE

Early stone and Gothic works are on the ground floor. Late Gothic, Renaissance and Baroque, and 19th-century works are on the first floor. The second floor has 20th-century exhibits, while the top floor has Hungarian works post 1945. The gallery also hosts a variety of fascinating temporary exhibitions.

portrays the women of the town defending Eger Castle against the Turks.

6 The Yawning Apprentice

Celebrated for its extraordinary detail, *The Yawning Apprentice* (1867) is a well-known and much-loved work by Hungary's finest Realist, Mihály Munkácsy.

7 Picnic in May

Painted from memory in 1873 by Pál Szinyei-Merse, *Picnic in May* is close to the French Impressionist style. The figure lying with his back towards the viewer is the artist himself.

8 Birdsong

Károly Ferenczy was one of Hungary's finest artists at the turn of the 19th century. *Birdsong*, painted in 1893, is one of his best works. It sees him move away from the "delicate naturalism" made famous by French artists and towards his own distinct style.

9 The Recapture of Buda Castle in 1686

Gyula Benczúr painted this large-scale historical masterpiece for the 1896 Millennium Celebrations. It was meant to emphasize the need for Austro-Hungarian rule by showing that Hungary was only freed from Turkish rule thanks to Karl of Lotharingia – leader of the forces that breached the castle walls – and Eugene of Savoy, who held up the army's rear.

10 Woman Bathing

Nudes were a speciality of Károly Lotz, who painted this sensuous figure in 1901. An example of academic painting, it evokes the style of the French artist Ingres. Lotz also painted the murals in the Parliament *(p22)*.

Benczúr's depiction of the liberation of Buda

Secession Works in the Gallery

***The Manor House at Körtvélye* (1907) by Rippl-Rónai**

1. Woman in a White-Spotted Dress

One of three important Secession artists, József Rippl-Rónai studied in Paris at a time when the Art Nouveau movement was starting to flourish. His masterpiece *Woman in a White-Spotted Dress* (1889) is widely considered the first Secession-style work painted in Hungary. It depicts the somewhat affected pose of a model apparently caught off-guard.

2. Woman with a Birdcage

An early painting by Rippl-Rónai, *Woman with a Birdcage* (1892) is well known for its great use of contrast – the white of the girl's hands against the blurred, dark background. The slightly contrived pose of the model holding the cage is a trademark of the artist.

3. The Golden Age

The second of Hungary's great Secessionist triumvirate, János Vaszary oscillated between Art Nouveau and Post-Impressionism. His best work is probably this 1898 rendition of a couple yearning for a lost paradise.

4. The Manor House at Körtvélyes

Rippl-Rónai visited Italy in 1904 and was fascinated by the decorative mosaics he saw in many homes. This 1907 work anticipates his shift from soft brushwork to bolder strokes, which would culminate in the paintings of his later years.

5. Fancy Dress Ball

Vaszary's brightly coloured 1907 painting, also known as *Masquerade Ball*, vividly portrays Budapest society with a touch of decadence.

6. Breakfast in the Open Air

This 1907 painting by Vaszary makes fabulous use of light and colour, and showcases the artist's bold brushwork. Ostensibly a flattering portrayal of a Budapest high society family at breakfast, the youngest child's troubled look suggests hidden problems and adds depth to the work.

7. The Garden of the Magician

The youngest of Hungary's Secessionist trio, Lajos Gulácsy was greatly influenced by his years in Italy, where he painted *The Garden of the Magician* (1906–7). His work also reflects the influence of the English Pre-Raphaelites.

8. Girls Getting Dressed

This 1912 Rippl-Rónai work shows the progression of his typical "corn kernels" style, where his brushstrokes became bolder and his colours brighter. The somewhat awkward pose of the girl on the left betrays the artist's love of playing with the viewer's perception.

9. Self-Portrait with Hat

Lajos Gulácsy's *Self-Portrait with Hat* (1912) reinforces his detached view of the world and, perhaps, his lack of belief in his own abilities. In the painting, he wears an anxious and vulnerable expression.

10. Riders in the Park

Vaszary's *Riders in the Park* (1919) showcases his use of sharp brushstrokes and high-contrast colours, clearly revealing the influence of Matisse, who he knew from his sojourns in Paris.

TOP 10
SECESSIONIST BUILDINGS

1. Four Seasons Hotel Gresham Palace *(p87)*
2. Gellért Hotel and Baths Complex *(p79)*
3. Museum of Applied Arts *(p92)*
4. Geology Institute *(Map F3)*
5. Hungarian National Bank *(Map K2)*
6. Post Office Savings Bank *(Map L2)*
7. Városliget Calvinist Church *(Map E3)*
8. Franz Liszt Academy of Music *(Map D3)*
9. New York Palace *(Map D4)*
10. New Theatre *(Map M2)*

THE SECESSION

Detail on the exterior of the Four Seasons Hotel

From its quiet beginnings among avant-garde artists in Vienna in the late 1880s to its expansion across Europe and ultimate decline in the 1920s (as Art Deco rose in its place), the Secession movement was an attempt to break away from the Romantic historicism of 19th-century art. The movement tried to find new inspiration in the distant past; in Hungary, it explored the bold colours of Transylvanian folk art. Common motifs also included floral designs directly inspired by Japanese art. Often characterized by fantastical designs, bright colours and stylized forms, the movement repossessed art from the nationalists. It encompassed all forms of the decorative and visual arts, from painting and sculpture to interior design. It is represented in the paintings of the National Gallery, in the Zsolnay ceramics allround the city, and many of the city's buildings.

Soaring glass ceiling at the Four Seasons Hotel Gresham Palace

7

MÁTYÁS CHURCH

H2 I, Szentháromság tér 2 9am–5pm Mon–Fri, 9am–noon Sat, 1–5pm Sun For mass and other events matyas-templom.hu

The profusion of architectural styles in Mátyás Church reflects the city's tumultuous history. The original church was destroyed in 1241 and a new church, part of Béla IV's fortified city, was built from 1255 to 1269. Much of this Gothic building remains, but it was Mátyás Corvinus, the church's namesake, who expanded it in the 15th century.

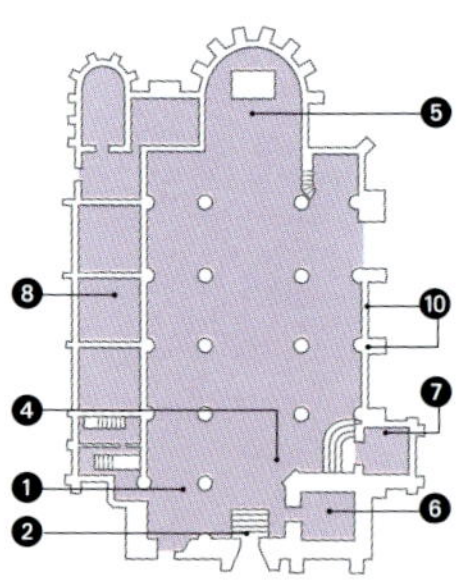

Mátyás Church Site Plan

1 Béla Tower

Named after the church's founder, Béla IV, the stout Béla Tower retains many of its original Gothic features, though the spire and turrets are all reconstructions. The tower is the least embellished part of the church.

2 Rose Window

The Neo-Gothic Rose Window over the main portal was recreated by Hungarian architect Frigyes Schulek after he found fragments of an earlier window during the 19th-century restoration of the church. The original had been bricked up after the liberation of Buda in 1686, when Jesuit fathers modified the church in the Baroque style.

3 Roof

The building's striking roof, decorated with multi-coloured glazed tiles, was added between 1950 and 1970. It replaced the original plain roof, which burnt down after Soviet shelling during the siege of Budapest in 1944–5.

4 Hidden Images of King Louis

Enter the church through the main portal, turn and look up to see the 14th-century images of King Louis the Great and his wife on the uppermost pillar beside the portal.

Diamond-patterned roof of the church

EAT
Ruszwurm *(p76)*, one of Budapest's most historic cafés, is just across the square and a short walk along Szentháromság utca. Be sure to order a classic strudel.

5 Altar

The early Gothic-style altar, in the shape of a cathedral, has a replica of the holy Hungarian crown atop a statue of the Virgin Mary. A shrine to the Madonna, it was designed by Schulek and completed in 1893.

6 Loreto Chapel and Baroque Madonna

Legend has it that in 1686, the Madonna appeared before the Turks defending Buda Castle, who saw it as a sign of imminent defeat. Habsburg troops took the castle that very night.

7 Mary Portal

A fine example of Gothic stone carving, this portal was rebuilt by Schulek in the 19th century using fragments of the original building.

8 Tomb of King Béla III and Anne de Châtillon

Schulek designed this elaborate tomb after the mortal remains of Béla III and his first wife were found during excavations at Székesfehérvár Cathedral in 1862.

9 Sunday Mass

A well-known centre of spiritual music, the church has two 1909 Rieger organs, considered the finest in Hungary, which are played during Sunday Mass. The church also hosts over 100 concerts a year.

KING MÁTYÁS

One of the greatest figures in Hungarian history, Mátyás is claimed by both Serbs and Romanians as one of their own. Born in Cluj-Napoca, in present-day Romania, he was the son of János Hunyadi, who in turn was the grandson of native Serbs. His origins are still a cause of tension between Hungarian and Romanian historians.

10 Stained-glass Windows

Designed by Frigyes Schulek and painted by Károly Lotz, the three windows on the church's southern side depict the Virgin Mary's life, the family of Béla IV and St Elizabeth of Árpádház, who was married at 13, widowed at 19 and died at 24.

Clockwise from right **Neo-Gothic Rose Window; elaborate stone carvings in the church; marble Tomb of King Béla III and Anne de Châtillon**

HUNGARIAN STATE OPERA

M2 VI, Andrássy út 22 Hours vary, check website opera.hu

Nowhere in Budapest is the ancient regime as alive and well as at the Hungarian State Opera, architect Miklós Ybl's magnum opus. A Neo-Renaissance masterpiece built in 1884, its roll call of musical directors reads like a who's who of central European music – Ferenc Erkel, Gustav Mahler and Otto Klemperer, among others.

TOP TIP

Visit Eiffel Art Studios, another venue of the State Opera, for more budget-friendly shows.

1 Façade

The passage of time has been kind to Adrássy Avenue *(p97)*, and the Hungarian State Opera is not as hemmed in as the city's other notable buildings. The opera features an impressive façade of colonnades, balconies and loggias.

2 Main Entrance

Stand under the building's sublime entrance with its muralled ceilings, and you will immediately wish you were part of 19th-century Budapest society, stepping out of a horse-drawn carriage to attend a premiere.

3 Statues of Liszt and Erkel

The busts of two of Hungary's greatest composers – Franz Liszt and Ferenc Erkel – stand guard on either side of the entrance. Both composers were sculpted in person by Alajos Stróbl, who was also responsible for much of the building's interior design.

Royal Box in the centre of the auditorium

Beautiful ceiling frescoes in the foyer

4 Foyer

The pretty foyer is a wonderful riot of murals, columns, chandeliers and gilded vaulted ceilings. Ostentation to rival Vienna was the order of the day, and Ybl did not disappoint his patrons.

5 Foyer Murals

Painted by Bertalan Székely and Hungarian Realist painter Mór Than, these murals cover the entire ceiling and depict the nine muses and other allegorical scenes.

6 Main Staircase

One of the opera's classic set pieces is a large chandelier hanging above marble stairs, which are covered by a red carpet. Its gilded ceiling panels are decorated with nine exquisite paintings by Mór Than, illustrating the awakening and triumph of music.

7 Royal Box

Ybl always insisted that the Royal Box was his finest achievement. With sculptures that symbolize the four operatic voices – soprano, alto, tenor and bass – it is set in the centre of a circle of three-tiered boxes.

8 Chandelier

Above the grand auditorium is a fine 2,722-kg (3-ton) Mainz chandelier illuminating a magnificent fresco by Károly Lotz of the Greek gods on Olympus. The chimney located above it facilitates ventilation.

9 Main Stage

The central stage of the opera was equipped with the most advanced technology of its time. During the construction of the opera house, the Vienna Ring Theatre was destroyed by fire. As a safety measure, an iron curtain and all-metal stage hydraulics plus a sprinkler system were installed here.

10 Museum

The museum houses memorabilia of famous performers who have graced this stage. Sándor Svéd, a renowned Hungarian baritone who performed at New York's Metropolitan for years, features prominently.

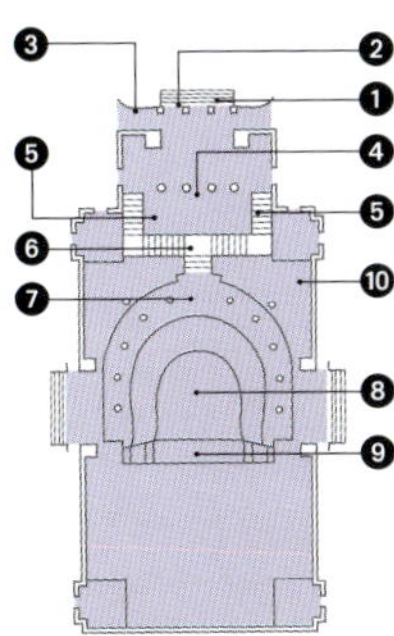

Hungarian State Opera Site Plan

HUNGARIAN NATIONAL MUSEUM

M5 VIII, Múzeum körút 14–1 10am–6pm Tue–Sun mnm.hu

Since its founding in 1802, the Hungarian National Museum has been home to the country's largest archive of art and artifacts, chronicling Hungary's history from the Roman era through to the fall of Communism in 1989. The building itself is a timeless piece of Neo-Classical architecture and the pièce de résistance of celebrated architect Mihály Pollack.

1 Diadem
Dating from the Hun period in the 5th century CE, this stunning gold diadem is the most ancient of its kind. Discovered in Csorna, it features 158 precious stones.

2 Sabretache Plate, Galgóc
This plate is considered one of the finest examples of the palmette ornamental style from the Conquest period, which began in 896 CE. In the shamanistic beliefs of the time, palmettes symbolized the Tree of Life.

3 Golden Stag
This hand-forged 38-cm- (15-in-) long Golden Stag dates from the 6th century BCE. Crafted from sheet gold with relief ornamentation, this Scythian artifact once adorned a prince's shield.

Golden Stag, a fine example of Scythian art

Impressive façade with a grand portico

4 Coronation Mantle

Originally a chasuble (a sleeveless outer vestment), the silk gown gifted by St Stephen in 1031 to a church in Székesfehérvár was adorned with figures of Christ and the Apostles. In the 13th century, it was refashioned into a mantle and thereafter worn by Hungarian kings for their coronations.

5 Monomachos Crown

The exquisitely crafted crown of Constantine IX Monomachos is made of gold plaques that date from between 1042 and 1050. The gold leaf is decorated with allegories of the Great Virtues, which were very popular in Byzantine art.

6 Funeral Crown

Discovered in 1838 in a church on Margaret Island, this 13th-century golden crown, decorated with lilies and rosettes, was worn by a female member of the Árpád family on her deathbed.

7 Processional Crucifix

Found in Szerecseny, this crucifix is similar to a piece in the St Stephen Museum in Székesfehérvár, suggesting the two are likely to have originated from the same workshop. In Hungary, many such crucifixes were found in churches destroyed during the Tatar invasion of 1241.

8 Mozart's Clavichord

Bought for the young Wolfgang Amadeus Mozart by his father, Leopold Mozart, this travelling clavichord was used by the Austrian child prodigy for practice during concert tours.

9 Electioneer-March in Front of the National Museum

As its title suggests, this pre-Secession painting by Franz Weiss shows the political campaigning of reformists and conservatives between 1847 and 1848. This was a time when, unlike most Western nations, Hungary was still characterized by feudalism.

FERENC AND ISTVÁN SZÉCHENYI

The National Museum may not have existed at all without the art and artifacts donated in 1802 by Count Ferenc Széchényi, who also established the National Library. His equally illustrious son, István, who frequently advocated for peasants, even paid for the country's first railway.

10 Red Engine

Painted by Sándor Bortnyik, this Cubist-style work is a fine example of activist art from the 20th century. Bold colours such as red and blue are contrasted with white to highlight the sense of movement.

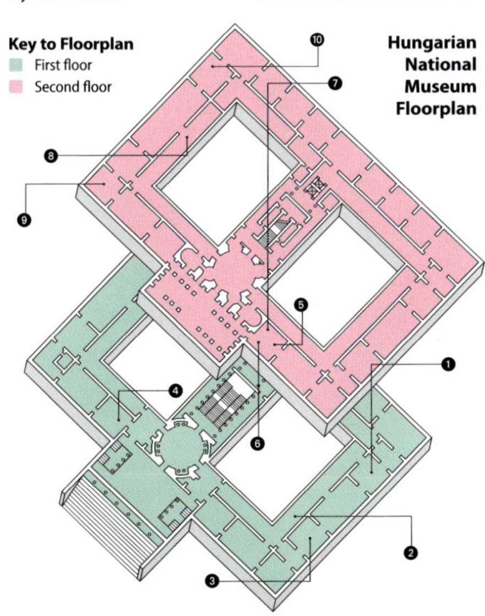

Hungarian National Museum Floorplan

GREAT SYNAGOGUE

D4 VII, Dohány utca 2 Hours vary, check website
jewishtourhungary.com

Europe's largest synagogue was built in a Byzantine-Moorish style to the designs of Viennese architect Ludwig Förster between 1854 and 1859. It can accommodate over 3,000 worshippers and includes a museum that is home to religious relics and Judaic devotional items, as well as a Holocaust Memorial.

1 Upper Galleries

When built, the highly ornamented upper galleries were designed for women who, according to tradition, had to worship separately. Today, all worshippers sit together downstairs.

2 Organ Concerts

The original 5,000-pipe organ – installed in 1859 and played by Franz Liszt during the synagogue's dedication ceremony – was replaced with a mechanical organ in 1996. Concerts are held throughout the summer.

3 Chandeliers

The two Spanish-style chandeliers above the main aisle are similar to those at the Hungarian State Opera: the design

Spanish-style chandeliers in the main chamber

EAT
Behind the synagogue on Síp utca 12 is the Kosher Deli *(kosherdelibudapest.hu)*, a restaurant and delicatessen that offers delicious Israeli kosher dishes.

Intricate detailing on the façade

was common in concert halls throughout Europe at the time.

4 Hungarian Jewish Museum

This museum *(p50)* is home to a collection of historical Judaica from ancient Rome to the 20th century. There's also a memorial dedicated to Raoul Wallenberg, who saved thousands during the Holocaust.

5 The Ark

Situated on the eastern wall facing the *bimah* (a platform used for services), the Ark contains a number of scrolls. These were salvaged from other synagogues and hidden by Hungarian Catholic priests from the Nazis during World War II.

6 Twin Towers, Onion Domes

The Great Synagogue was the first in Europe to feature towers. They are 43-m- (140-ft-) high and topped with golden Byzantine domes.

7 Inscription Above the Main Entrance

Engraved in gold over the entrance is a verse in Hebrew from the book of Exodus: "And let them make me a sanctuary that I may dwell among them."

8 Rose Window

Above the main entrance, the façade features a spectacular rose window, with a Star of David motif, which is reminiscent of the architecture found in Hungary's medieval churches.

9 The Ten Commandments

Two stone tablets sit atop the synagogue. They resemble the shape of the building and are engraved in Hebrew with the Ten Commandments.

10 Menorah Paving

A menorah is depicted on the ground in front of the synagogue. Most visitors focus on the building, so it often goes unnoticed.

RAOUL WALLENBERG

Swedish diplomat Raoul Wallenberg saved as many as 100,000 Hungarian Jewish people during 1944–45, mainly by issuing them with Swedish travel documents. In 1945, Wallenberg was arrested as a spy by the Soviet Union and taken to Moscow's Lubianka Prison, where he died in 1947. The Israeli government declared him "Righteous Among the Nations" in 1996. A memorial in his honour stands on the corner of Szilágyi Erzsébet fasor and Nagyajtai utca.

TOP 10 OF EVERYTHING

Statue of King Stephen I at Fisherman's Bastion

HISTORIC SITES

1 Parliament

Built in the Gothic Revival style between 1885 and 1904, this magnificent structure *(p22)* dominates the Danube's eastern bank. Its soaring spires, elaborate façade and ornate interior (complete with sumptuous staircases and stained-glass windows) are symbolic of Hungary's grand aspirations during the Austro-Hungarian era. The building also houses the Holy Crown of Hungary, which can be viewed on a guided tour (book online in advance).

2 Széchenyi Chain Bridge

The first permanent bridge linking Buda and Pest, this bridge *(p53)* is the engineering marvel that consolidated Budapest's unification. Designed by English engineer William Tierney Clark and completed in 1849, it managed to survive heavy Nazi attacks in 1945 and remains an icon of the city today – the stone lions guarding each end have become symbols of the city's resilience.

3 Liberty Square (Szabadság tér)

This politically charged square is home to some of Budapest's most controversial monuments, including the last remaining Soviet War Memorial (which dates from 1945 and honours Red Army soldiers). Statues of Ronald Reagan and US World War I general Harry Hill Bandholtz, who is remembered for preventing occupying Romanian military authorities from removing artifacts from the Hungarian National Museum, are also on display in the square.

Statue of Ronald Reagan in Liberty Square

4 Buda Castle (Royal Palace)

Initially built in the 13th century, this UNESCO World Heritage Site (also known as the Royal Palace) has been destroyed and rebuilt multiple times. The current Baroque complex *(p73)*, reconstructed after World War II bombing, houses the Hungarian National Gallery *(p34)* and Budapest History Museum. Its strategic hilltop position offers commanding views over the Danube.

5 Fisherman's Bastion

Constructed between 1895 and 1902, this neo-Romanesque terrace *(p74)* on the edge of Castle Hill is one of Budapest's most-photographed landmarks. Its fairy-tale turrets (of which there are seven) represent the seven Magyar tribes that settled in the Carpathian Basin from 896 CE *(p8)*. There are numerous theories about the origin of the bastion's name, the most famous being that the complex was dedicated to the Guild of Fishermen, who were responsible for the upkeep of this section of the castle wall in the medieval era.

6 Hungarian National Museum

Hosting an expansive collection that traces thousands of years of Hungarian history, this acclaimed museum is one of the country's best. It has another claim to fame, however. In 1848, the museum *(p42)* played a key role in the Hungarian Revolution: the uprising was partially triggered by the reading of Sándor Petőfi's "12 points" (including a demand for an indepen-

Exploring Heroes' Square and Millenium Monument

dent Hungarian government) and the famous patriotic poem *Nemzeti dal* ("National Song") on the front steps of the museum.

7 Shoes on the Danube

This haunting memorial *(p53)* of 60 pairs of cast-iron shoes along the Pest embankment commemorates Jews murdered here by the fascist Arrow Cross militia in 1944–45 (victims were forced to remove their shoes before being shot into the Danube). The installation was created by sculptors Gyula Pauer and Can Togay.

8 Memorial of Unity (Trianon Memorial)

K1 Alkotmány u 2

Inaugurated in 2020 opposite the Parliament building, this controversial memorial commemorates the centenary of the 1920 Treaty of Trianon, when Hungary lost two-thirds of its territory. The 100-m (330-ft) underground ramp displays the names of 12,537 settlements from pre-Trianon Greater Hungary, ending at an eternal flame which represents enduring national solidarity.

9 Heroes' Square and Millennium Monument

Created for Hungary's 1896 millennium celebrations, this grand plaza *(p98)* features the Archangel Gabriel set atop a soaring column and surrounded by statues of the Seven Chieftains of the Magyars. The colonnades display Hungary's greatest kings and leaders, making it a stone chronicle of a thousand years of history.

10 House of Terror Museum

Housed in the former headquarters of both Nazi and Communist secret police, this thought-provoking museum *(p99)* chronicles Hungary's darkest 20th-century chapters. The building's history is preserved through original interrogation rooms and holding cells, alongside torture tools, serving as a powerful memorial to political oppression.

Exhibits inside the House of Terror Museum

MUSEUMS AND GALLERIES

1 Hungarian Ethnographic Museum

This remarkable building *(p99)* showcases the cultural heritage of central Europe through a range of permanent exhibits, focusing on farming, textiles and technology. It also hosts temporary exhibitions throughout the year.

2 Hungarian Jewish Museum

M4 VII, Dohány utca 2 10am–8pm Mon–Thu & Sun, 10am–4pm Fri Sat & Jewish hols milev.hu

Budapest's Jewish community is based around the Great Synagogue *(p44)*, and the Hungarian Jewish Museum can be found in a wing to the left of the synagogue's main entrance. Established in 1931, it is home to thousands of historic relics and religious items. There is also a room devoted to the Holocaust and, in the courtyard, a memorial to the 600,000 Hungarian Jewish people who were killed by the Nazis.

Ritual object in the Hungarian Jewish Museum

3 Hungarian National Museum

Founded on the personal collection of philanthropist Count Ferenc Széchenyi, the National Museum *(p42)* has been home to a stunning array of Hungarian artifacts since 1802. The building is a masterpiece in its own right.

4 House of Music

Designed by Japanese architect Sou Fujimoto, the House of Music *(p30)* offers a fascinating visual and aural tour through the history of both Hungarian and world music. It features concert halls, an open-air stage, exhibition spaces and the SoundDome, a vast 3D cinema with a 360-degree projector.

5 Castle Museum

Set in the labyrinthine rooms of the Royal Palace, this museum *(p73)* can be tricky to navigate. Do persevere, as it gives great insights into the history of the city. The museum's real strength, however, is in covering the story of the castle itself, starting with the ruins of the medieval structure in the basement.

6 Museum of Fine Arts

Housed in a Neo-Classical building, the Museum of Fine Arts *(p97)* has a fine collection of pieces from all artistic eras and genres. Raphael,

Exquisite Romanesque Hall in the Museum of Fine Arts

Toulouse-Lautrec, Picasso and Goya all feature, and there are also collections of ancient Egyptian and Greek art.

7 Hungarian National Gallery

Over 10,000 exhibits make the Hungarian National Gallery's *(p34)* collection one of the best in the world. Spread across the Royal Palace, Hungarian works of art from medieval times to the present are displayed here.

8 House of Terror Museum

This thought-provoking museum *(p98)* tells the harrowing tale of State terror carried out by Hungary's Fascist and Communist dictatorships. There are grim reconstructions of prison cells and torture chambers. The museum also serves as a memorial to the thousands killed by the totalitarian regimes.

9 Vasarely Museum

P1 III, Szentlélek tér 6 10am–6pm Fri–Sun vasarely.hu

Born Győző Vásárhelyi, Victor Vasarely was the founder of the Optical Art movement in Paris in the 1930s. This museum, based in the Zichy Palace, is dedicated to his life and work. It also hosts temporary exhibitions of 20th-century art.

10 Ludwig Museum Budapest – Museum of Contemporary Art

P2 IX, Palace of Arts, Komor Marcell utca 1 10am–6pm Tue–Sun ludwigmuseum.hu

This museum is known for its refreshingly vibrant display of modern Hungarian art. More than 150 works dating from 1960 onwards document the progression of Hungarian artists as they attempted to break out of Socialist Realism. There are also a number of works by international contemporary artists. Note, the exhibitions change regularly.

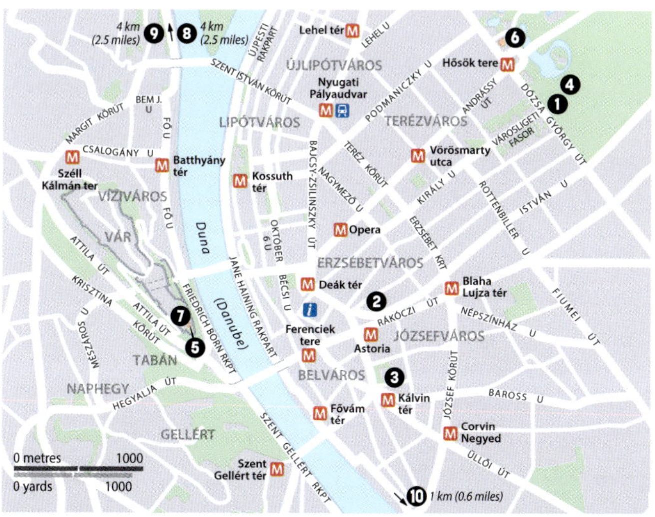

DANUBE SIGHTS

1 River Cruises

K4

Several companies run tours along the Danube in the summer months. The vast majority of tours depart from Vigadó Square *(p91)*. Mahart Passnave *(mahartpassnave.hu)* operates evening cruises – including drinks and dinner – to Vienna, too. There are also hydro-foil services to Vienna twice a week, running from the end of April to the end of September.

2 Hungarian Parliament

Rising dramatically from the Danube's east bank, the Hungarian Parliament *(p22)* appears at its best when viewed from the opposite bank of the Danube. Its design was inspired by Britain's Palace of Westminster, which was constructed in the 19th century in the Gothic Revival style.

3 Elizabeth Bridge

K5

Hailed as the longest suspension bridge in the world when completed in 1903, Elizabeth Bridge (Erzsébet híd) had to be completely rebuilt after World War II, and did not reopen until 1963. Great care was taken on the Pest side to ensure that the Inner City Parish Church *(p91)* was not damaged during rebuilding. At one point, the church's continued existence was threatened, with the bridge-builders and the Communist authorities wanting to demolish it, however, a compromise was reached and today the roadway passes just inches from the church's walls.

4 Margaret Island

A green oasis in the middle of the Danube, Margaret Island *(p32)* is the perfect spot to spend summer after-noons. It originally comprised three separate islands: Painter's Island (Festő), Bather's Island (Fürdőző) and

Cruising on a tourist boat on the Danube

Rabbit's Island (Nyúl-sziget). All three islands were later connected after extensive embankment work in the late 19th century helped to regulate the river's flow.

5 Margaret Bridge

B2

The gateway to Margaret Island, this bridge (Margit híd) was built by a Frenchman, Ernest Gouin, from 1872 to 1876, and is distinguished by its unusual chevron shape. The approach road to the island, however, wasn't added until the 1890s.

6 Liberty Bridge

Originally built in 1894–99, the Liberty Bridge (Szabadság híd) was destroyed by the Nazis during World War II, but an exact replica was built a few years later. This famous bridge *(p82)*, adorned with legendary Hungarian *turul* birds atop its Modernist girders, was formerly known as Emperor Franz József Bridge until the Communists later opted for a less imperial name.

7 Castle Hill Funicular

H3 I, Buda Castle, Clark Ádam tér 7:30am–10pm daily 1st and 3rd Mon of every month bkv.hu

One of the best ways to reach Castle Hill is by hopping on this 19th-century funicular. The journey is short, the cabins tiny, but the views of the Danube as well as the city spread out below are absolutely breathtaking.

8 Embankment Walk

B3, B4, C5

This walk, offering excellent views of the city's most popular sights, extends along most of the Pest embankment, from Liberty Bridge to Margaret Island and beyond. Several boats moored on the various quays have cafés aboard, including Boatanic *(boatanic.hu)* and Spoon *(spoonboat.hu)*.

9 Chain Bridge

J3

Completed in 1849, the iconic Chain Bridge (Széchenyi lánchíd) was the first permanent crossing over the Danube between Buda and Pest. On either side of the bridge are two huge towers that support the mammoth chains from which the bridge takes its name. Impressive at any time of day, the bridge is particularly spectacular when lit up at night, making it one of the city's most-photographed sights. In summer, the bridge closes on weekends to host a cultural festival.

10 Shoes on the Danube

J2

This moving memorial was created by sculptors Gyula Pauer and Can Togay in 2005, and comprises 60 pairs of cast-iron shoes lined up at the edge of the Pest embankment, just south of the Hungarian Parliament building. The site had been used as a place of execution by Fascist Arrow Cross militiamen, who shot hundreds of Jewish people here in 1944–45.

***Shoes on the Danube*, a poignant memorial to Holocaust victims**

BATHS AND SWIMMING POOLS

1 Gellért Hotel and Baths Complex

Of all Budapest's baths, Gellért *(p79)* is perhaps the finest, but is closed for renovation until 2028. It offers a great network of mineral-rich thermal baths and the outdoor pools feature one of the world's first artificial wave machines.

2 Lukács Baths

B2 II, Frankel Leó út 25–9 6am–10pm daily lukacsfurdo.hu

Opened in 1894, the Neo-Classical Lukács Baths offer three outdoor swimming pools, as well as three indoor thermal pools, along with Kneipp baths, a fitness room, sauna and mud treatments.

3 Dagály Medicinal Baths and Strand

P1 XIII, Népfürdő út 36 6am–7pm daily nsu.hu

Located some way from the city centre, Dagály Strand is Budapest's largest pool complex, comprising 10 pools, including a few children's pools, plus a hydrotherapy and fitness centre.

4 Széchenyi Baths

Set in a building designed by the architect Győző Czigler in City Park, the Széchenyi Baths *(p97)* offer a range of thermal water treatments. The mineral-rich springs are known for their alleged healing properties, in particular for treating disorders of the nervous system, joints and muscles.

5 Magnolia Day Spa

J2 V, Zoltán utca 3 Noon–8pm Wed–Fri, 10am–8pm Sat & Sun magnoliadayspa.hu

This spa in the heart of Budapest uses only natural ingredients and offers over 100 types of massages, as well as body and facial treatments, manicures and pedicures.

6 Rudas Baths

K5 I, Döbrentei tér 9 Hours vary, check website rudasfurdo.hu

Built by the Turks in the 16th century, the Rudas Baths are among the oldest in the city. There are six steam pools and a swimming pool.

7 Hajós Alfréd National Swimming Pool

B1 XIII, Margaret Island 6am–7pm daily nsu.hu

Designed by architect and sportsman Alfréd Hajós, who represented Hungary

at the 1896 Olympic Games in swimming and football, the three sports pools here (including an Olympic-sized one) are still used by the national swimming team for training.

8 Palatinus Strand

P1 XIII, Margaret Island 9am–7pm daily palatinus strand.hu

Budapest's most popular swimming complex has water slides, pools and hot springs.

9 Veli Bej Bath

B2 II, Árpád fejedelem útja 7 6am–noon & 3–9pm daily irgalmasrend.hu

Built in 1574, this Turkish bath has five thermal pools of varying temperatures, a jacuzzi, steam cabins, saunas, a Kneipp bath, massage showers, a swimming pool and a range of wellness services. Note that only over-14s are allowed.

10 Ensana Thermal Margaret Island

B1 Margaret Island 7am–9pm daily ensanahotels.com

Budapest's most exclusive baths can be found at the opulent Ensana Thermal Margaret Island hotel *(p119)*.

Soaking in the mineral-rich thermal pools at Széchenyi Baths

TOP 10 BATH TIPS

Enjoying a water jet massage

1. Massage
Almost all baths and pools offer various forms of massage at an extra cost. Try one to relax and rejuvenate yourself.

2. Payment
The price list, posted at the entrance to all the baths, is usually several pages long. The entrance fee depends on the service you choose and is valid for a day. Last admission is an hour before closing time.

3. Towels
Bring your own towel, or hire one for a fee plus an additional deposit.

4. Sheets to Cover Yourself
In baths where men and women bathe together (such as the Rudas Baths), use the small sheet you'll be given.

5. Lockers
Most baths have secure lockers where you can leave all your valuables for a small fee.

6. Water Temperature
All baths display the temperature of the water by the side of the pool.

7. Steam Rooms
Entry to the steam room – where there is one – is usually included in the standard entrance fee.

8. Etiquette
Most thermal baths are unisex. In single-sex baths and facilities swimming costumes are optional.

9. Wave Pools
Gellért, Dagály and Palatinus Strand all have artificial wave machines.

10. Family Bathing
Children are welcome in most of the city's baths, but the thermal baths do not admit anyone under 14 years old.

OFF THE BEATEN TRACK

1 Kiscelli Museum

P1 III, Kiscelli utca 108 10am–6pm Tue–Sun kiscelli muzeum.hu

While the exhibitions at the Kiscelli Museum offer a fascinating look at the history of Budapest over the past three centuries, the main attraction here is the stunning building itself. Perched atop a wooded hill, the elegant 18th-century former monastery showcases a mix of architectural styles.

2 People's Park

Locals say that City Park, or Városliget, is for tourists, while real Budapesters head for Népliget, or People's Park *(p104)*. Built to celebrate the 1873 unification of Buda, Óbuda and Pest, the park is peppered with statues and monuments, and is also home to a planetarium, which is currently undergoing renovation.

3 Lehel Market

D2 XIII, Lehel tér Daily lehelcsarnok.hu

A bit of an eyesore from the outside, this is nevertheless the market to visit if you want a local shopping experience. Keep an eye out for farmers selling fresh produce direct from their own plots, as well as a huge range of delicious homemade cheeses.

4 Lukács Baths

Though not as celebrated as some of the better-known bath houses in Budapest, Lukács Baths *(p54)* offer a local experience. The ticketing system is complicated and you may need an English-speaking local to help, but it all adds to the impression that you are far from the tourist crowds here. Prices are much lower, too.

5 Mikszáth Kálmán Square and Budapest VIII

D5 VIII, Mikszáth Kálmán tér

Even just a decade ago, this square, along with much of the historic Budapest VIII district, was something of a no-go area for tourists. However, private investment in its handsome yet long-neglected buildings has rejuvenated the whole area, and it now has an appealing bohemian vibe, with funky shops, chic galleries and a buzzing nightclub scene. In summer, the square is a great place to people-watch, with locals and visitors both enjoying the café terraces.

6 Tomb of Gül Baba

B2 II, Mecset utca 14 10am–6pm daily gulbaba alapitvany.hu

Gül Baba was a Muslim dervish, poet and philosopher who died in 1541, just after the fall of Buda. His remains now lie in this simple tomb built between 1543 and 1598, and a statue of him stands nearby. Surrounded by a rose garden, the tomb is engraved with golden quotations from the Qur'an. It is a short but steep walk to the tomb from Margaret Bridge.

The 400-year-old tomb of Gül Baba

Ruins of the ancient Roman city of Aquincum

7 Aquincum

It's a pity that Aquincum *(p103)*, one of the largest Roman sites in central Europe, is not more popular with visitors to Budapest. Wandering its ancient streets, lined with the remains of formerly grand temples, shops and houses, is a joy, especially early in the morning, when you may have the place to yourself.

8 Pálvölgy Caves

These caves *(p105)* are less well known than the more accessible Szemlő-hegyi Caves *(p103)* for good reason. The most spectacular sights at Pálvölgy can be reached only via steep ladders and by navigating tricky natural rock formations as part of a 3-hour tour with an experienced guide.

9 Holocaust Memorial Center

The interactive multimedia exhibition at this centre *(p93)* tells the story of Hungary's Jewish and Roma communities during the Holocaust. Exhibits here include newsreels, photographs and personal and religious items. The centre is situated on the grounds of the restored 1924 Páva Street Synagogue, which houses a memorial wall engraved with the names of all those who lost their lives during the Holocaust.

10 Fő Square, Óbuda

P1

The focus of Fő Square, in the suburb of Óbuda, is the splendid Zichy Palace, built for the Zichy family and now home to museums dedicated to the avant-garde works of Victor Vasarely and Lajos Kassák. The Neo-Baroque Fő Square Palace opposite is perhaps even more impressive, while just north of the square on Laktanya utca is a group of statues, *Women with Umbrellas*, by contemporary sculptor Imre Varga. Just up ahead is the Imre Varga Collection, where further examples of the sculptor's work can be seen.

FAMILY ATTRACTIONS

Castle Hill funicular trundling its way up a steep incline

1 Flipper Museum

C2 VIII, Radnóti Miklós utca 18 4–11pm Wed–Fri, 2–11pm Sat, 10am–10pm Sun flippermuzeum.hu

This wacky museum is home to a treasure-trove of over 130 pinball machines, from late 19th-century examples to state-of-the-art pinball tables from the 21st century, almost all of which can be played. There is also a selection of old video games, as well as foosball and air hockey tables.

2 Capital Circus

E2 XIV, City Park (Városliget), Állatkerti körút 12/a Shows: daily fnc.hu

A theatrical experience not to be missed, this permanent circus offers plenty of fun for the entire family. The programme varies, but the focus is on remarkable feats of acrobatics, light and water shows, high-wire acts and colourful clowns. In summer, the circus hosts the International Circus Festival. Shows are over two hours long, so may tire small children.

3 Castle Hill Funicular

Visitors of all ages adore riding in the front cabin of the Castle Hill funicular *(p53)* even though it's a short journey that takes three minutes or so.

4 Palatinus Strand

Margaret Island is home to Palatinus Strand *(p55)*, Budapest's most popular swimming pool and thermal bath complex. Slides and a variety of children's pools make it a popular choice among families.

5 Csopa – Center of Scientific Wonders

E3 III, Bécsi út 38-44 10am–7pm daily csopa.hu

Hungary's first hands-on science exhibition, Csopa offers a playful learning experience for all ages. Delve into the world of physics with over 100 live science shows and exhibits, or enter Nature's Workshop and try activities such as Hover Over the Earth.

6 Budapest Zoo

E2 XIV, Városliget, Állatkerti körút 6–1 Hours vary, check website zoobudapest.com

Budapest's zoo is large, well funded and one of the best in the region. It has a large aquarium, an impressive aviary and a superb reptile house. The zoo also has one of Europe's best animal welfare, adoption and wildlife protection programmes.

7 Labyrinth

G2–G3 I, Úri utca 9 11am–6pm daily labirintus.eu

Older children will love exploring this underground maze of tunnels and chambers. It is thought that the caves, which are around 15 m (49 ft) below ground level, were formed by hot

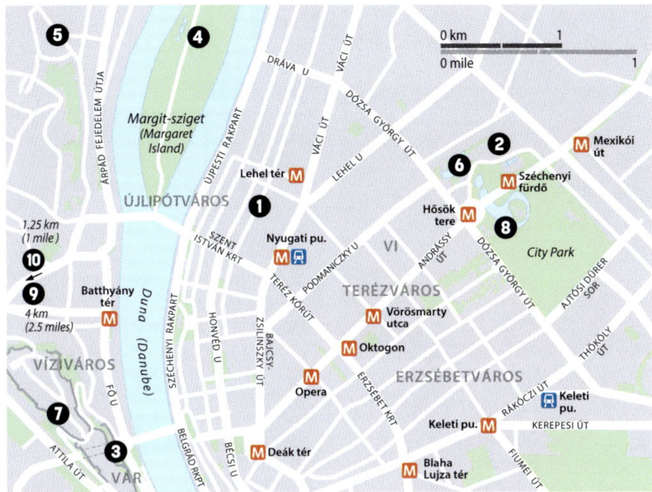

springs about half a million years ago. They were a refuge for hunters and gatherers from around 10,000 BCE, and even served as a bomb shelter during World War II. A special exhibition on the infamous prisoner Vlad Tepes, also known as Dracula, includes a torture chamber and mannequins of his victims.

8 Open-air Ice-skating Rink and Boating Lake

E2 City Park (Városliget)
Hours vary, check website
mujegpalya.hu

In winter, City Park Lake turns into a skating rink, where people ice-skate to classical music. During summer, boats replace skaters, as families row their craft around the lake. Skates and boats can both be hired at the jetty near the pavilion. There is also a visitors' centre.

9 Children's Railway

N1–N2 XII, Golfpálya út
9am–4pm daily (last trains vary)
gyermekvasut.hu

Children aged 9 to 14 operate a narrow-gauge railway that passes through the Buda Hills *(p103)* from Széchenyi Hill to Hűvös Valley. The only adults on board are the engineers. To get to the train, take the Cogwheel Railway *(bkk.hu)* up from Városmajor.

10 Memento Park

Young history buffs will enjoy this impressive open-air museum *(p104)*, which combines gargantuan statues of the likes of Vladimir Lenin and Karl Marx with a hands-on, interactive exhibition dedicated to Hungary's Communist past. There's also the chance to take a ride in a Trabant – an iconic Communist-era car – and shop for Soviet-style memorabilia in the gift shop.

Enjoying the open-air ice-skating rink, City Park

LOCAL DISHES

Traditional stuffed cabbage rolls

1 Stuffed Cabbage (Töltött Káposzta)

A hearty dish of cabbage leaves filled with minced meat and rice, often served during holidays. This dish reflects Hungary's resourceful culinary tradition and the influence of neighbouring cuisines.

2 Goulash (Gulyás)

The quintessential Hungarian dish, goulash is more than just a stew; it's a cultural icon. This rich, hearty soup was first eaten by cattle herders to stay nourished and warm while on the go. It is made with beef, vegetables, and, of course, a generous amount of Hungary's national spice, paprika. A must-have for any visitor.

3 Lángos

Commonly found at street food stalls and markets, particularly during festivals, *lángos* consists of fried dough typically topped with sour cream and cheese.

4 Chicken Paprikash (Paprikás Csirke)

Arguably Hungarian home cooking at its finest, this comforting, creamy chicken dish is cooked with paprika and served with *nokedli* (small dumplings). The combination of tender chicken in a velvety paprika sauce works wonderfully.

5 Fisherman's Soup (Halászlé)

This traditional river-fish dish, a speciality along the Danube and Tisza rivers, is often enjoyed on Christmas Eve in Hungary. It's fairly spicy, with an intense paprika flavour and deep red colour.

6 Dobos Torte (Dobos Torta)

Created by József Dobos in 1884, this five-layer sponge cake with chocolate buttercream and a caramel top showcases the country's sophisticated pastry tradition and innovative culinary history.

Cold fruit soup, or *gyümölcsleves*

7 Cold Fruit Soup (Gyümölcsleves)

This refreshing soup of chilled fruit with sour cream combines some of the best of Hungary's seasonal produce. It is often served as a light starter or a dessert, and you'll find that every household has their own version.

8 Cottage Cheese Pasta (Túrós Csusza)

A simple but delicious pasta dish of cottage cheese and sour cream topped with crispy bacon. *Túrós csusza* is another wonderful example of elevating humble ingredients into delectable comfort food.

9 Chimney Cake (Kürtőskalács)

This sweet, spiral pastry roasted over charcoal is an icon of Hungary's street dessert culture. Its theatrical preparation and cinnamon-sugar coating make it a favourite among visitors and locals alike.

10 Pörkölt with Nokedli

Often confused with goulash, this meat stew has a thicker sauce and is served with egg noodles or dumplings. The paprika adds a depth of flavour, making this a warming everyday Hungarian dish.

A busy street-food stall offering up *lángos*

TOP 10 HUNGARIAN DRINKS

1. Pálinka
The Hungarian word for fruit brandy, *pálinka* is distilled from fruits grown in the orchards situated on the Great Hungarian Plain.

2. Unicum
Originally prescribed as a remedy for the king by court physician Dr Zwack, this liqueur is made with more than 40 herbs.

3. Pezsgő
Hungary's top-quality sparkling wine is often made using indigenous grape varieties and a traditional production method similar to that of champagne.

4. Fröccs
This refreshing fizzy drink is the perfect way to cool down during hot summers. It is made by mixing wine with *szódavíz* (carbonated water).

5. Szódavíz
Invented by Hungarian scientist Ányos Jedlik, *szódavíz* is a true national drink, available at several pubs. It costs less than bottled mineral water.

6. Bikavér
Known as Bull's Blood, this dry red wine blend is produced from grapes ranging from garnet red to deep ruby.

7. Sör
Some of the best known Hungarian *sör* (beer) brands are Dreher, Soproni and Borsodi.

8. Puszta koktél
Traditional cocktail of Hungary, *puszta koktél* is made with Tokaji *szamorodni* wine, apricot brandy, Mecsek liqueur and lemon oil or sour cherry.

9. Szörp
A homemade local fruit and herb syrup, often used to make drinks in some bars.

10. Tokaji aszú
Hungary's legendary dessert wine is said to be one of the earliest and finest examples of botrytized wine.

SHOPS AND MARKETS

1 WestEnd City Center

C2 VI, Váci út 1–3 8am–10pm daily westend.hu

This vast, three-level complex of more than 400 shops is located next to Nyugati Railway Station. All your favourite brands and stores can be found here, though don't expect great bargains, as prices are often high. The complex also has plenty of restaurants and cafés, as well as a rooftop garden, for when you want to take a break from shopping. Some community events also take place here.

2 Palais Herend

K3 V, József nádor tér 10–11 10am–6pm Mon–Fri, 10am–2pm Sat herend.com

As much a museum as it is a shop, Palais is an authorized retailer of Hungary's finest porcelain, Herend. The Herend factory, west of the city, has been making exquisite porcelain for generations. Most pieces featuring the Apponyi floral pattern design command high prices. They are housed in large, priceless wooden cabinets beneath a splendid wooden ceiling.

3 Fashion Streets

K3 & L2–L3

Classy fashion stores and cafés dominate two of the city's most elegant shopping streets – Deák Ferenc utca and Andrássy Avenue *(p97)*. Deák Ferenc utca (also called Fashion Street), which runs towards Váci Street, features brands such as Hugo Boss and Tommy Hilfiger. More glamorous options line the elegant Andrássy Avenue, including Louis Vuitton and Gucci.

4 Central Market Hall

M6 V, Vámház körút 1–3 Hours vary, check website piaconline.hu

Budapest's main produce market is great for local delicacies. Impeccably

Stalls at the bustling Central Market Hall

clean, it has numerous stalls selling meat, salami, fruit and vegetables. The upper floor has street-food stalls, restaurants and souvenir shops.

5 BÁV Jewellery (Rubin Ékszerbolt)

L4 V, Párizsi utca 2 10am–6pm Mon–Sat bav-art.hu

Choose from a selection of fine antique watches and jewellery at one of the country's best-known auction houses. There are several other BÁV shops across the city, specializing in a variety of different items.

6 Polgár Galéria

M4 V, Kossuth Lajos utca 3 10am–5pm Mon–Fri, 10am–12:30pm Sat polgar-galeria.hu

Polgár is a sensational art and antiques gallery where you can purchase works by both classical and contemporary Hungarian artists. You will also find rare antiques, including imperial Habsburg furniture, here. The gallery even takes care of all onward shipping and related paperwork.

7 Rózsavölgyi Szalon Arts & Café

L4 Szervita tér 5 10am–8pm Mon–Sat szalon.rozsavolgyi.hu

Rózsavölgyi is a treasure-trove for music lovers. Opened in 1912, the store specializes in sheet music and records, but sells musical instruments, too. It is also a venue for theatrical and musical performances and literary and fine arts events, which you can enjoy along with a cup of coffee or a light meal.

8 Allee

XI, Október Huszonharmadika utca 8–10 9am–7pm daily (to 8pm Sun) allee.hu

Located on the Buda side of the Danube, Allee is a modern, pet-friendly shopping mall where visitors can find almost anything ranging from clothing and electronics to restaurants and cafés. It is popular with both locals and visitors. Many large stores are clustered here and it is easily accessible from the city centre by public transport.

9 WAMP – Design in the City

C4 & A2 wamp.hu

Held occassionally on weekends in two locations – Erzsébet tér and Millenáris Park – the WAMP design fair provides young Hungarian designers with an opportunity to sell handmade items, including textiles, jewellery and kitchenware. There are also stalls selling homemade delicacies.

10 Memories of Hungary

L3 V, Hercegprímás út 8 10am–10pm daily memoriesofhungary.hu

Located next door to St Stephen's Basilica *(p26)*, Memories of Hungary sells artifacts made by local craftspeople and artists. Pick up a souvenir from their wide range of fabrics, porcelain, ceramics, toys, food items, jewellery and Rubik's Cubes®. The store has several locations throughout the city.

Handcrafted ceramics on sale at Memories of Hungary

BUDAPEST FOR FREE

1 Shoes on the Danube

This poignant memorial *(p53)* features a collection of 60 cast-iron shoes commemorating the Jewish people who were ordered to remove their footwear before being executed here. A sombre reminder of the city's dark past, this moving display can be seen along the banks of the Danube, between Parliament *(p22)* and the Academy of Sciences *(p86)*.

2 Museums on National Holidays

Entry to most of Hungary's state and municipal museums is free on national holidays *(p67)*. The Hungarian National Gallery *(p34)*, the National Museum *(p42)* and the Museum of Fine Arts *(p97)* are the pick of the bunch. Note that the guided tour of Parliament *(p22)* is not free.

3 Walking Tours

Budding tour guides and locals keen to share their knowledge of the city offer a number of free, themed daily walking tours during spring and summer. The unofficial meeting point is the fountain in Vörösmarty Square *(p91)*: get there between 10am and 11am and you should have no problem finding one to join. Although free, your guide will appreciate a tip if you find the tour worthwhile.

4 Danube Carnival

Throughout June, the Danube Carnival takes over Vörösmarty Square, the Pest Embankment and – on some weekends – the Chain Bridge. Most of the concerts, parades, street art and children's events in the festival are free.

5 Gellért Hill

Climbing the steep incline of Gellért Hill *(p82)* to reach the Citadel *(p80)* at the top can be a challenge even for the fittest. Make sure to stop and admire the Gellért Monument *(p80)* on the way up, before heading down the other side via the Cave Church *(p79)*.

6 Fisherman's Bastion

The turrets of the Fisherman's Bastion *(p74)* on Castle Hill offer a spectacular bird's-eye view of all the city's major landmarks. Just make sure you get here early in the morning, as the crowds can get somewhat overwhelming later on.

Iconic Chain Bridge with the Pest Embankment in the backdrop

7 City Park

Central Budapest's largest park *(p96)* offers a wide range of things to see or do for free, from admiring the Millennium Monument on Heroes' Square to enjoying a walk through its surprisingly densely forested paths. The park also has a large number of flower beds around the central lake, a riot of colour in bloom.

8 Margaret Island

Elegant Margaret Island *(p32)*, a park since the 1860s, is where Budapest residents come to find some peace and quiet. Walk from one end to the other, past the ruins of a 13th-century Dominican monastery, a UNESCO-protected water tower and through a lush Japanese Garden, all for free.

9 Inner City Parish Church

While Mátyás Church across the river gets all the attention and visitors (despite the steep entrance fee), most locals agree that the free Inner City Parish Church *(p91)* is even more impressive. Look out for remains of the original 15th-century frescoes, as well as the *mihrab*, a reminder of Budapest's Turkish occupation.

10 Pest Embankment

A walk along the Danube embankment *(p53)* is an insightful trip through various eras of Hungarian history and architecture, all overseen by the Royal Palace on the opposite bank. Look out for street artists and musicians in summer.

TOP 10 BUDGET TIPS

Bottles of local wine

1. Local Hungarian beer and wine is usually cheaper than imported alcohol, and often tastes much better.
2. Most restaurants in the city centre – especially those close to office buildings – offer cheap yet delicious set menu deals at lunchtime.
3. Pack a picnic basket and head to either of Budapest's main parks, People's Park (Népliget) and City Park (Városliget), to enjoy a lovely, lazy lunch.
4. Look out for free concerts and street performers in Vörösmarty Square and along Váci Street.
5. Most hotels in Budapest tend to offer lower rates during the week.
6. Budapest's smarter hostels usually have private rooms with bathrooms, and are much cheaper than hotels.
7. Buy a travelcard if using public transport. These are available for one, three or seven days and make travel much cheaper *(bkk.hu)*.
8. Do what local pensioners do and visit bath houses early in the morning to grab the lowest prices.
9. The Budapest Card *(budapest-card.com)* offers free public transport and reduced-price admission to several museums and a number of other attractions.
10. The city's yellow licensed taxis have fixed rates. Make sure the price per kilometre is clearly displayed.

FESTIVALS AND EVENTS

1 Budapest Dance Festival

W tancfesztival.hu

Hosted by the National Dance Theatre and Hungary's cultural hub, the Palace of Arts, this annual festival (usually held in late February) is a grand celebration of dance. It features the premiere of the season's newest productions and brilliant performances by both Hungarian and international artists and dance companies. The event also honours the year's best Hungarian artists with awards.

2 Budapest Spring Festival

W btf.hu

The Budapest Spring Festival runs for two weeks in April and features world-class performers. Outstanding opera, chamber and classical music, literature and theatre take over almost every performance art venue in the city.

3 Budapest Summer Festival

W szabadter.hu

From June to August each year, the open-air Budapest Summer Festival takes place every weekend. The city's parks and Margaret Island *(p32)* transform into an imaginative stage during this time for performances of theatre, opera, ballet and concerts by both international and Hungarian artists.

4 Hungarian Grand Prix

W hungaroring.hu

Hundreds of thousands of fans flock to the Hungaroring circuit, about 19 km (12 miles) outside of Budapest to witness a thrilling race (usually held in July). Tickets are expensive and best booked in advance.

5 Sziget Festival

W sziget.hu

Central Europe's biggest pop and rock festival makes perfect use of Óbudai, an island in the middle of the Danube. The week-long event, held in mid-August, attracts some of the world's leading artists. Most revellers stay on the island the whole week, sleeping in tents.

6 Festival of Folk Arts

W mestersegekunnepe.hu

For four days in August, Dísz tér in the Castle District comes alive with arts and crafts stalls as skilled craftspeople from all over Hungary arrive to showcase and sell their wares. There are also folk music and dance performances. Highlights include the folk art parade that takes place on St Stephen's Day (20 Aug).

7 Jewish Summer Festival

W iemj.org

This week-long celebration of Jewish culture, usually held at the end of

Folk dancers at the Budapest Spring Festival

August, features music, dance, visual arts, comedy and cabaret. For details, visit the Jewinform kiosk next to the Great Synagogue *(p44)*.

8 Budapest Wine Festival

W aborfesztival.hu

Every September, the area around Buda Castle is filled with Hungary's finest wine merchants and artisanal food producers, who display their latest offerings. There is also a parade and a charity wine auction.

9 CAFe Budapest Contemporary Arts Festival

W cafebudapestfest.hu

"Art is communication; communication can best be learned through art" – this is the motto that drives this festival, held in mid-October. One of Europe's leading celebrations of the contemporary arts, it showcases the work of artists who have few opportunities open to them, and aims to stimulate communication among proponents of different genres.

10 Christmas Fair

At the end of November, Vörösmarty Square turns into a merry market for Hungarian arts, crafts and food. At 5pm daily, a new window of the Advent calendar opens on the façade of Gerbeaud Cukrászda *(p94)*.

Festive Christmas market in Vörösmarty Square

TOP 10

PUBLIC HOLIDAYS

1. Anniversary of 1848 Revolution (15 Mar)
Hungarians pay their respects to the famous poet and revolutionary Sándor Petőfi by re-enacting his poem at the National Museum *(p42)*.

2. Easter (Mar/Apr)
As a largely Catholic nation, Hungarians celebrate Easter quietly at home.

3. Whit Sunday and Monday (7th Sunday and the following Monday after Easter)
This national holiday celebrates the descent of the Holy Spirit upon the Apostles.

4. Labour Day (1 May)
Once a Communist holiday marked with processions of workers, Labour Day is still observed as a national holiday in the country.

5. St Stephen's Day (20 Aug)
A brilliant fireworks display over the Danube celebrates the coronation of St Stephen (István), Hungary's patron saint.

6. Republic Day (23 Oct)
A double celebration commemorates the outbreak of the 1956 Revolution and the 1989 proclamation of the Republic of Hungary.

7. All Saints' Day (1 Nov)
On this day, saints who do not have their own holy days are celebrated. The preceding day, people visit cemeteries to light candles in remembrance of their lost relatives.

8. Santa Claus Day (6 Dec)
Children leave their shoes on the window sill for Santa Claus (Mikulás) to fill with sweets and toys.

9. Christmas (24–26 Dec)
The city's famed Christmas market comes alive with food, crafts and music throughout December.

10. New Year (31 Dec)
New Year's Eve is celebrated on the streets. Vörösmarty Square usually hosts concerts and firework displays.

DAY TRIPS FROM BUDAPEST

1 Visegrád

40 km (25 miles) N of Budapest **visegrad.hu**

A popular tourist destination, Visegrád is located on the narrowest stretch of the Danube. It is famous for its 13th-century ruined castle, which sits atop a hill overlooking the town, with its massive outer walls still intact.

2 Gödöllő

30 km (19 miles) NE of Budapest

The 18th-century Grassalkovich Mansion *(kiralyikastely.hu)* in Gödöllő is best known for its open-air concerts and theatrical performances.

3 Fót

25 km (16 miles) NE of Budapest

Fót is home to Károlyi Palace, the birthplace of Hungary's first president, Mihály Károlyi. The palace was the work of famed architect Miklós Ybl, who also designed the town's attractive Church of the Immaculate Conception.

4 Kecskemét

86 km (53 miles) SE of Budapest **kecskemet.hu**

Ödön Lechner's town hall (1893–96), with pink tiles and minaret-like spires, is Kecskemét's biggest draw. Another fine building is the Secession-style Cifra Palace *(kkjm.hu/cifrapalota)*, built as a casino in 1902.

5 Ráckeve

43 km (27 miles) SW of Budapest **tourinformracheve.hu**

This town's principal attraction is its Orthodox church, the oldest in Hungary. It was built by Serb settlers in 1487. The interior walls are covered with beautiful frescoes.

6 Kiskunfélegyháza

110 km (68 miles) SE of Budapest **kiskunfelegyhaza.hu**

Nationalist poet Sándor Petőfi spent part of his childhood in this town, and

Pastel-coloured buildings lining a street in Szentendre

his house is now a museum, which also houses archaeological and ethnographical exhibits. East of the town is the Kiskunfélegyháza National Park *(knp.hu/en)*, a popular spot for birdwatchers.

7 Vác

40 km (25 miles) N of Budapest tourinformvac.hu

Destroyed and then rebuilt in the 17th century, this medieval town is known for being the site of Hungary's Arc de Triomph, built in 1764.

8 Martonvásár

30 km (19 miles) SW of Budapest martonvasar.hu

Martonvásár is home to the stately Brunswick Palace, which has a history of reconstruction. Rebuilt in the grand Baroque style in the 18th century, it was again reconstructed a century later in the Neo-Gothic style. Little of the original now remains, barring the splendid parklands around, which are still much as they originally were. The estate's church, built in 1775, also remains largely unaltered. The interior of the church is decorated with well-preserved frescoes.

9 Esztergom

46 km (28 miles) NW of Budapest esztergom.hu

The capital city from the 10th to 13th centuries and the site of St Stephen's baptism and coronation, Esztergom is the country's most sacred city. The vast basilica *(bazilika-esztergom.hu)* here, built in the 19th century, is the seat of Roman Catholicism in Hungary.

Nave framed by arches at the basilica in Esztergom

10 Szentendre

25 km (16 miles) N of Budapest szentendre.hu

With cobbled lanes, pastel-coloured buildings and tall Orthodox church spires, Szentendre is a picturesque Hungarian town. The Hungarian Open Air Museum *(skanzen.hu)*, which showcases country life from the 18th century until World War I, and the Ferenczy Museum's Margit Kovács Ceramics Exhibition *(femuz.hu/en/museums)*, which displays the works of one of Hungary's best ceramic artists, both draw a huge number of tourists.

AREA BY AREA

Picturesque street in Budapest

THE CASTLE DISTRICT AND NORTH BUDA

Medieval Buda grew around its 13th-century castle, which sits atop a hill overlooking the Danube. This historic area features winding lanes lined with traditional cafés and restaurants and is home to some of the city's top sights, including the Royal Palace and Mátyás Church. North of the castle is Víziváros (Water Town), once home to those too poor to live on Castle Hill, but now one of the city's most exclusive residential districts.

For places to stay in this area, see p116

1 Royal Palace

B4 Szent György tér
budacastlebudapest.com

Towering above Budapest, the Royal Palace, also known as Buda Castle, is an amalgamation of several buildings. Most of the present structure was built in the 18th century during the reign of Maria Theresa, but it was preceded by a palace and two castles. The first castle was built around 1255, then it was rebuilt by Mátyás I in 1458. Following damage in World War II, the palace was renovated again, with some parts, such as the dome, being entirely rebuilt. It now houses several museums, including the Castle Museum and the Hungarian National Gallery.

2 Castle Museum

J4 I, Wing E of the Royal Palace, Szent György tér 2 10am–6pm Tue–Sun varmuzeum.hu

This fascinating collection of artifacts and historical documents traces the city's and the castle's history via three distinct exhibitions. The basement houses a display on the castle during the Middle Ages, including a re-creation of a vaulted chapel from the 1255 structure. Gothic sculptures and armour that were unearthed while renovating the Royal Palace after World War II are also displayed. The ground floor has exhibits on the city's evolution from Roman times to the 17th century, and the first floor explores "Budapest in Modern Times". The museum is part of the wider

Artworks on display in the Hungarian National Gallery

Budapest History Museum, which also includes Aquincum *(p103)*, so locals often call it by that name.

3 Hungarian National Gallery

It would take weeks to view all the exhibits in the Hungarian National Gallery *(p34)*, as there are thousands of works on display at any given time. From medieval altarpieces to striking Secession paintings, it's all here. The gallery shares its collection with the Museum of Fine Arts *(p97)*.

4 Sándor Palace

H3 I, Szent György tér 1–3
To the public

The official residence of the Hungarian president can only be admired from the outside, but the superb Neo-Classical motifs and bas-reliefs by Richárd Török, Miklós Melocco and Tamás Körösényi are worth spending time over. The palace was commissioned in 1806 by Count Vincent Sándor and designed by Mihály Pollack and Johann Aman. It was severely damaged in 1944, and was almost entirely rebuilt after World War II.

Royal Palace on Castle Hill overlooking the Danube

Statues along a stairway in Fisherman's Bastion

5 Fisherman's Bastion

H2 I, Halászbástya, Szentháromság tér 24 hours daily

Designed in the Neo-Romanesque style by Frigyes Schulek as a monument to the Guild of Fishermen in 1895, Fisherman's Bastion resembles a fairy-tale castle. Perched on the edge of Castle Hill, its turrets and terraces offer the most picturesque views of Pest.

6 Lords' Street

G2 I, Úri utca

Baroque and Gothic façades give Lords' Street (Úri utca) its unique medieval character, though most of the houses were rebuilt from 1950 to 1960, after being destroyed during World War II. The street runs the full length of Castle Hill and its highlights include the Hölbling House at No 31, with its sublime Gothic façade, the Telephony Museum at No 49 and the bizarre but exceptional Labyrinth *(p58)*, whose entrance is at No 9. The real highlight, however, is just the walk from one end to the other.

THE ANONYMOUS ALAGÚT

The tunnel (alagút) that runs through Castle Hill was one of the later projects of Adam Clark, the Scottish engineer who built the Chain Bridge *(p53)*. Clark settled in Budapest after completing the bridge. The square that faces the tunnel's entrance on the Danube side bears his name. The tunnel itself, 350 m (1,150 ft) long and 11 m (36 ft) high, remains unnamed.

7 Vienna Gate Square

G1 I, Bécsi kapu tér

The Vienna Gate you see today is, in fact, a replica of the original structure, which once led from Buda towards Vienna. The replica was built in 1936 to celebrate the 250th anniversary of Buda's liberation from the Turks. Gothic and Baroque houses line the sides of the square. The huge building on the square's left-hand side is the Hungarian National Archive, a Neo-Romanesque structure famous for its multicoloured roof.

8 Batthyány Square

H1 I, Batthyány tér

Set in the heart of Víziváros, this square is named after Count Lajos Batthyány, the prime minister during the Hungarian Uprising of 1848–49. Though marred by traffic, the square is full of architectural wonders. The Hikisch House at No 3 has bas-reliefs of the four seasons, and St Anne's Church is a fine Baroque building. A monument to Ferenc Kölcsey, who wrote the words of the national anthem, overlooks the square.

Ribbed vaulted ceiling at Mátyás Church

9 Church of St Mary Magdalene

G2 I, Kapisztrán tér 6
10am–6pm daily

Built in the 13th century for the city's Hungarian citizens, who were forbidden from praying at Mátyás, this church now lies in ruins. All that remains is the tower and gate – the rest of the building was pulled down after World War II. Nevertheless, the site is enchanting, and the square in which it stands is unusually peaceful.

10 Mátyás Church

Standing on the site of a 13th-century structure, Mátyás Church *(p38)* was rebuilt and named after King Mátyás in 1470. Through most of the Middle Ages, Hungarians were not permitted in the church; only Germans could worship here. It has witnessed several significant events, from the marriage of Mátyás to the coronations of Franz József I and Charles IV. Béla III and his wife are also buried here. When the Turks came to power in the early 1500s, they converted Mátyás Church into a mosque. According to legend, in 1686, a statue of the Madonna appeared before the Turks while they were praying. They took this as a sign of defeat and surrendered the city of Buda to the Habsburgs. The church was also the scene of fierce fighting during World War II, and was not renovated until 1968.

A DAY IN THE CASTLE DISTRICT AND NORTH BUDA

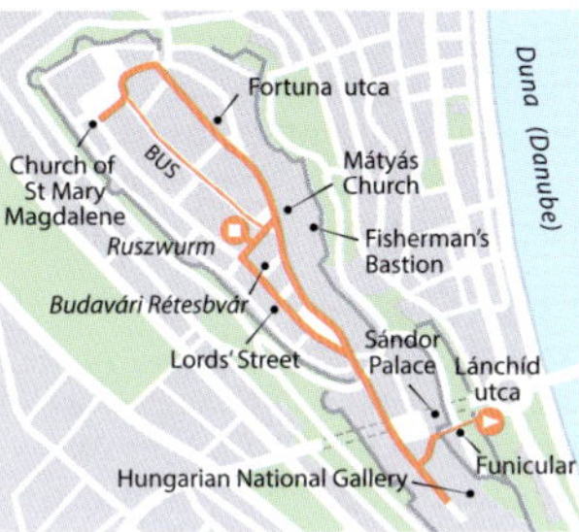

Morning

There's no better way to get up to the castle than by taking the **funicular** *(p53)* from Lánchíd utca. At the top, admire the stately **Sándor Palace** *(p73)* from the outside. On the other side of the palace is the superb **Hungarian National Gallery** *(p34)*. It would be easy to spend all day here, but with careful planning you should be able to see the highlights within an hour or so. Next, stroll along the castle ramparts to **Lords' Street**, with its charming Baroque and Gothic buildings, and end with a relaxing lunch at **Budavári Rétesbvár** *(p76)*.

Afternoon

Head eastwards to **Fisherman's Bastion** and enjoy fabulous views of the Danube and Pest on the opposite bank. Next door is the historic **Mátyás Church**. If you are lucky, you may even get to enjoy a concert here. You can stock up on souvenirs at the shops on **Fortuna utca** – the Hilton Budapest hotel *(p116)* has a superb souvenir shop – before following the road to the ruins of the **Church of St Mary Magdalene**. From the church, take the little Castle District bus back along Lords' Street to **Ruszwurm** *(p76)* for a cake or strudel.

Cafés, Pubs and Bars

1. Henri Belga Söröző

H2 I, Bem rakpart 12 Noon–midnight daily belgasorozo.com

This pub, located next to a restaurant of the same name, serves more than 20 types of beer.

2. Ruszwurm

G2 I, Szentháromság utca 7 Summer: 10am–7pm daily; winter: 10am–6pm daily ruszwurm.hu

Established in 1824, this family-run café is renowned for its delicious strudel and priceless period furniture.

3. Angelika

H1 I, Batthyány tér 7 Apr–Oct: 9am–midnight daily; Nov–Mar: 9am–11pm daily angelikacafe.hu

Housed in a former crypt of St Anne's Church, this historic patisserie serves superb pastries.

4. Korona Kávéház

H3 I, Dísz tér 16 10am–6pm daily koronakavehaz.hu

Savour delicious coffee and homemade cakes at this traditional café run by the same people that manage Ruszwurm.

5. Royal Guard Café

H3 Hunyadi udvar 11am–9:30pm daily foorseg.hu

Housed in the Royal Palace's former guard house and riding hall, this café offers coffee, drinks and light meals. It also features an exhibition showcasing guard costumes through the centuries.

6. Faust Wine Cellar

G2 1014, Hess András tér 1–3 2–5pm Mon, 5–8pm Thu, 2–8pm Fri–Sun gbwine.eu

Indulge in wine and *pálinka* (fruit spirit, p61) tastings at this cellar and buy your favourites by the bottle.

7. Calgary Antik Drink Bar

B2 II, Frankel Leó utca 24 06 30 847 34 72 4pm–4am daily

A cross between an antique shop, bar and club, the Calgary attracts crowds long after most places have closed.

8. Budavári Rétesbvár

G2 I, Balta köz 4 8am–8pm daily budavariretesvar.hu

This traditional Hungarian café is well known for its mouthwatering strudel, cheese scones and other delicacies.

9. Café Gusto

B2 I, Frankel Leó utca 12 8am–11pm Mon–Sat gustocafe.hu

Opened in 1992, this café offers a range of Italian coffees, generous platters, and a good selection of wines and spirits.

10. Oscar American Cocktail Bar

G1 I, Ostrom utca 14 5pm–3am Wed–Sat oscarbarbudapest.hu

Visit this sophisticated, movie-themed bar to try a fantastic range of cocktails, either shaken or stirred.

Patrons enjoying alfresco dining at Ruszwurm

Restaurants

Elegant interior of the posh Arany Kaviár

PRICE CATEGORIES

For a three-course meal for one, with half a bottle of wine (or equivalent meal), taxes and extra charges.

F under Ft7,500 **FF** Ft7,500–Ft12,500 **FFF** over Ft12,500

1. Arany Kaviár

G1 I, Ostrom utca 19 6–11pm Tue–Sun aranykaviar.hu • FFF

The era of the Russian tsars is conjured up with caviar, blinis and champagne in truly opulent surroundings.

2. Pest-Buda Bistro

G2 Fortuna utca 3 7:30am–10pm daily pest-buda.com • F

Known for its delicious Hungarian food and excellent local beer, Pest-Buda is the perfect spot to enjoy a good-value meal in the Castle District.

3. Pavillon de Paris

H2 I, Fő utca 20 Noon–11pm daily pavillondeparis.hu • FF

This French restaurant specializes in seafood and features a beautiful terrace and garden.

4. Stand25

G3 I, Attila út 10 Noon–4pm & 6–11pm Mon–Sat stand25.hu • FFF

This elegant restaurant serves contemporary Hungarian cuisine, such as veal meatloaf with split pea puree.

5. Halászbástya Étterem

H2 Halászbástya Noon–midnight Mon–Sat halaszbastya.eu • FFF

Enjoy the very best views of Pest and some of the city's finest food in an elegant Neo-Romanesque setting.

6. Baltazár

G2 I, Országház utca 31 8am–11pm daily baltazarbudapest.com • FF

Sample simple yet delicious and good-value food, including locally sourced steaks, burgers, duck and chicken, here. Grab a table on the cobbled street outside in summer.

7. Hungarian Kitchen/21

G2 I, Fortuna utca 21 Noon–midnight daily 21restaurant.hu • FF

Here you'll enjoy a contemporary twist on Hungarian cuisine. The dishes are cooked using fresh market produce.

8. Marischka

G2 Attila út 99 Noon–midnight daily (to 10pm Sun) marischka.hu • FF

This dog-friendly restaurant offers a contemporary take on Hungarian cuisine, plus a great wine list and some of the city's best cocktails. It's beautifully located, too, and has a spacious terrace.

9. Kacsa Vendéglő

B3 I, Fő utca 75 Noon–3pm & 5–11pm daily kacsavendeglo.hu • FFF

A variety of inventive duck dishes, served with a dramatic flair, makes Kacsa Vendéglő a popular spot.

10. Café Pierrot

G2 I, Fortuna utca 14 11:30am–11pm Wed–Sun pierrot.hu • FF

Founded as Budapest's first private café-restaurant in 1982, this delightful spot has great food and service.

GELLÉRT AND TABÁN

It is believed that Gellért Hill, which rises 140 m (460 ft) on the western bank of the Danube, was the scene of Bishop Gellért's death. In 1046, he was thrown from the top by enraged citizens for trying to convert them to Christianity. The hill was later the site of the Habsburgs' monumental Citadel, built to quell revolt. At the foot of the hill, the lavish Gellért Hotel and Baths Complex is a reminder of a gentler age. Tabán was once the city's most bohemian district, full of bars and gambling dens. More recently, urban planners have created parks and residential areas that now command some of the highest prices in the city.

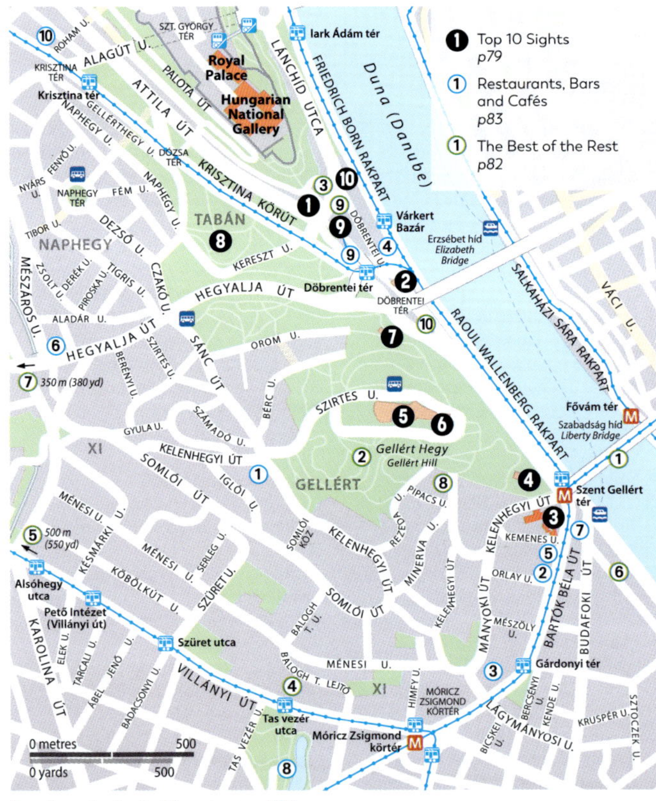

For places to stay in this area, see p116

Bronze monument of Queen Elizabeth of Hungary

1 Golden Stag House

J4 I, Szarvas tér 1 11:30am–10pm daily aranyszarvasetterem.hu

This distinctive early 19th-century house, at the foot of Castle Hill, was named after the inn here – "Under the Golden Stag". A superb bas-relief above its entrance depicts a golden stag pursued by a pair of hunting hounds.

2 Queen Elizabeth Monument

J5

Although Elizabeth (Erzsébet), wife of Habsburg emperor Franz József, was not Hungarian by birth, she adored her adopted subjects. A number of streets, bridges and monuments throughout the nation are named after her. The monument dedicated to her that overlooks the Danube from the Gellért embankment was designed by György Zala and erected in 1932. Its original home was on the other side of the river, but it was removed by the Communists in 1947 and reinstated at its present site in 1986.

3 Gellért Hotel and Baths Complex

L6 XI, Kelenhegyi út 4

Closed for renovation until 2028

gellertbath.hu

Built in 1918, these are the most luxurious baths in Budapest. The main pool is a Neo-Classical masterpiece. In summer, the open-air swimming pools at the back are popular with chess-playing pensioners. Although the baths are attached to the Gellért Hotel, their entrance is on the side street.

4 Cave Church

K6 I, Szent Gellért rakpart 1

9:30am–7:30pm Mon–Sat

sziklatemplom.hu

This remarkable place of worship, hewn into the Gellért hillside, was founded by monks of the Pauline Order after they visited Lourdes, France, in 1926. In 1951, the Hungarian secret police arrested the monks, murdering their leader Ferenc Vezér and sentencing the others to prison. The church was then bricked up and forgotten until August 1989. The revived order once again presides over the church now, which is closed to the public when services are in progress.

Cave Church carved into the slopes of Gellért Hill

Liberation Monument towering over the Citadel

5 Citadel

J6–K6

Although built to intimidate the citizens of Budapest after the failed uprising of 1848–49 and to prevent further revolts, the Citadel was never actually used for its original purpose, as the Hungarians sought their independence by more peaceful means. The country was granted partial independence according to the Dual Monarchy agreement of 1867, however, Austrian forces continued to occupy the fortress until 1897. The building is currently undergoing renovation to enhance visitor experience, but its lookout points remain accessible and offer some spectacular views of the city.

BISHOP GELLÉRT

In the 11th century, Bishop Gellért was thrown off Old Hill in a sealed barrel. To seek God's forgiveness, the citizens of Budapest decided to dedicate the hill to him a century later. The Bishop had been invited to Hungary to help the newly baptized St Stephen (István) spread Christianity in the region. It was rumoured that Prince Vata, Stephen's brother, had a hand in the martyrdom.

6 Liberation Monument

K6

One of the most visible landmarks in Budapest, this imposing cenotaph towers above the nearby Citadel. It was sculpted by Zsigmond Kisfaludi Stróbl and inaugurated in 1947 to commemorate the liberation of Budapest from Nazi Germany by Soviet forces. The inscription on the plinth once paid tribute to the Red Army, but was changed in 1992 to honour all those who "laid down their lives for Hungarian prosperity". Originally, a 6-m- (20-ft-) tall sculpture of a Soviet soldier equipped with a machine gun, with one of his fists clenched and the other holding a flag, stood at the foot of the monument, but this was later removed and relocated to Memento Park *(p104)*.

7 Gellért Monument

J5

According to legend, the city's patron saint Bishop Gellért was pushed off the hill that now bears his name for attempting to convert Budapest's citizens to Christianity, including young Prince Imre, the son of Stephen I (István). Constructed in 1904, the monument to this Christian martyr is now looking a little worse for wear, although it still retains its original majesty when viewed from afar. It is especially striking at night, when it is superbly lit. The statue and the huge Neo-Classical colonnade that flanks it were designed by Gyula Jankovits and Imre Francsek.

8 Tabán

H4

This was one of the first inhabited areas of Buda thanks to its ideal location, nestled between two hills near the Danube. The Celtic Eravi were the first to make a settlement here in 1000 BCE. The Romans later built a watchtower here and, in the 16th century, the Turks built the Rác Baths. In the 17th century, Tabán was home to Serb refugees, Greeks and Roma. In 1910, the narrow streets of Tabán on the slopes of Gellért Hill were cleared to make way for terraces, gardens and Secession buildings. Today, the district is a popular venue for summer concerts, while in winter, the hillside is ideal for tobogganing.

9 Tabán Parish Church

J4 I, Attila út 11 Hours vary, check website tabani.plebania.hu

The parish church is all that remains of Tabán's old district. Topped by a fine Neo-Baroque tower, it was built from 1728 to 1736 on the site of an earlier church that was converted into a mosque and later destroyed in the battle to overthrow the Ottoman Empire. Inside is a copy of the 12th-century carving, *Christ of Tabán*; the original is in the Castle Museum *(p73)*.

10 Miklós Ybl Square

J4 I, Ybl Miklós tér

Arguably Hungary's greatest architect, known for gems such as St Stephen's Basilica *(p26)* and the Hungarian State Opera *(p40)*, Miklós Ybl is honoured with a commemorative statue, which stands in a square bearing his name. It was designed by Ede Mayer and erected here in 1894, three years after Ybl died.

Bronze statue of Miklós Ybl

A DAY IN GELLÉRT AND TABÁN

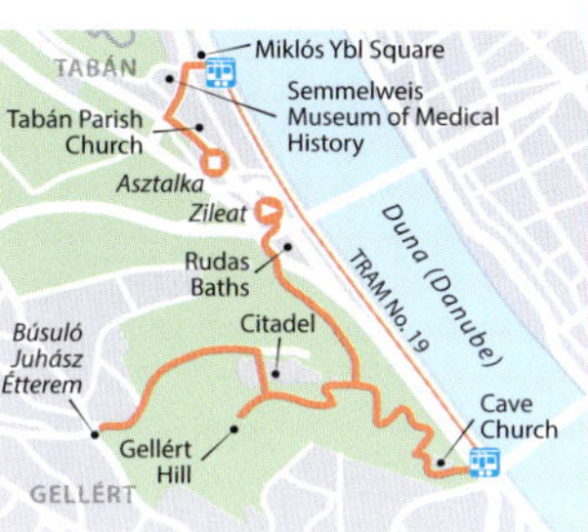

Morning

Start the day with coffee and breakfast at **Zileat** *(Döbrentei utca 22)* before walking a short distance along the embankment to the historic **Rudas Baths** *(p54)*. Try to resist the temptation to spend all day in the thermal baths and swimming pools. Once refreshed, you'll be in fine form to tackle **Gellért Hill** *(p82)* and climb up to the **Citadel**. Enjoy the views from its ramparts, then break for lunch at **Búsuló Juhász Étterem** *(p83)*.

Afternoon

After lunch, descend southwards to the **Cave Church** *(p79)*, hewn into the rock face of Gellért Hill. From here, stroll down to Gellért Square and travel north along the embankment on the splendid tram No 19 to **Miklós Ybl Square**. A short walk west leads you to the district of **Tabán**, where you'll be surrounded by Secession buildings. Next, visit the **Tabán Parish Church** just off Attila út, one of the few surviving buildings from Tabán's old district. To the north is the fascinating **Semmelweis Museum of Medical History** *(p82)*. End the day with a classic cake and a cup of coffee at **Asztalka** *(p83)* on Dobrentei utca.

Iconic Liberty Bridge, linking Buda and Pest

The Best of the Rest

1. Liberty Bridge

L6

Built between 1894 and 1899 by János Feketeházy, this bridge stands out with its bright green colour and decorative lion and *turul* (mythical bird) statues.

2. Gellért Hill

J6

The observation terraces on Gellért Hill provide a beautiful panorama over southern Buda and the whole of Pest.

3. Semmelweis Museum of Medical History

J4 I, Apród utca 1–3 10am–6pm Tue–Sun semmelweismuseum.hu

The house of the groundbreaking doctor Ignáz Semmelweis, now a museum, chronicles the history of medicine, from ancient Egyptian times to the present day.

4. Cistercian Church of St Imre

B6 XI, Villányi út 25 06 1 611 01 07

A Neo-Baroque gem built in 1938, this church holds the relics of St Imre, patron saint of the Cistercian Order.

5. Sas Hill Nature Reserve

N2 XI, Tájék utca 26 Hours vary, check website dunaipoly.hu

This small reserve is a biodiversity hotspot. Its visitor centre has information on the rare plants, insects and reptiles found here, including the Pannonian lizard.

6. University of Technology and Economics

C6 XI, Műegyetem rakpart 3 bme.hu

Hungary's largest academic institution was built in 1904. Its alumni include Ernő Rubik, the inventor of the well-known Rubik's Cube®.

7. Budapest Congress Center

A5 XII, Jagelló út 1–3 For events only bcc.hu

Established in 1975, this arts complex houses the Novotel Budapest Hotel and conference rooms. It hosts concerts and major exhibitions.

8. Former Swedish Embassy

K6 XI, Minerva utca 3 To the public

This building was made famous by Swedish diplomat Raoul Wallenberg *(p45)*, who saved thousands of Jewish prisoners from Nazi death camps. A monument to him stands nearby.

9. Virág Benedek Building

J4 Apród utca 10 2–6pm Wed, Fri & Sat; 10am–6pm Sun museum.hu

The only remnant of the old Tabán area, which was detroyed by fire in 1810, this place now hosts temporary exhibitions.

10. Rudas Baths

The famous Rudas Baths *(p54)*, covered with a Turkish-style dome, are among the oldest in the city, dating from around 1550.

Restaurants, Bars and Cafés

1. Búsuló Juhász Étterem

B6 XI, Kelenhegyi út 58 Noon–11pm Tue–Sun busulojuhasz.hu • FFF

This traditional Hungarian restaurant on the slopes of Gellért Hill specializes in game dishes.

2. KEG Sörművház

C6 Orlay utca 1 Noon–11pm Mon–Wed & Sun, noon–midnight Thu–Sat kegsormuvhaz.hu • FF

There are over 30 ales on tap at this craft beer pub, along with a good selection of traditional dishes.

3. La Nube

C6 XI, Bartók Béla út 41 5–11pm daily (from noon Sat & Sun) lanubecafe.com • FF

This tapas and wine bar serves platters of fine cheese, cold meats and seafood. There are plenty of vegan options, too.

4. Zileat Brunch & Bistro

J4 I, Döbrentei utca 22 8:30am–9pm daily (from 9am Sat & Sun) zileat.hu • F

At Zileat, a fabulous range of brunch dishes is served alongside homemade cakes in a bright and colourful setting.

5. Szeged Étterem

C6 XI, Bartók Béla út 1 Noon–11pm daily szegedvendeglo.hu • FF

A Hungarian restaurant near the Gellért Hotel, Szeged Étterem serves mouthwatering river-fish dishes.

Elegant dining room of Búsuló Juhász Étterem

PRICE CATEGORIES

For a three-course meal for one, with half a bottle of wine (or equivalent meal), taxes and extra charges.

F under Ft7,500 **FF** Ft7,500–Ft12,500 **FFF** over Ft12,500

6. János Étterem

A5 XI, Hegyalja út 23 Noon–11pm daily janosetterem.hu • FFF

A surprisingly good restaurant in a rather nondescript hotel, János Étterem has a menu mainly made up of Hungarian classics.

7. Palack Borbar

K6 XI, Szent Gellért tér 3 Noon–midnight Tue–Sat, noon–10pm Sun & Mon palackborbar.hu • FF

This spot serves tasty homemade cakes and unique coffee blends. It also has an excellent selection of wines.

8. Hemingway Étterem

P2 XI, Kosztolányi Dezső tér 2 Noon–midnight daily (to 4pm Sun) hemingway-etterem.hu • FF

Escape the bustle of the city with a refreshing mojito or a cigar on the terrace at this exceptional seafood restaurant.

9. Asztalka

J4 I, Döbrentei utca 15 06 20 581 33 99 11am–6pm Wed–Fri, 11am–7pm Sat & Sun • F

This busy café offers an ever-changing selection of scrumptious cakes alongside a choice of gourmet coffees.

10. Déryné Bisztró

G3 I, Krisztina tér 3 Hours vary, check website deryne.com • FF

Popular with locals, this family-friendly, French-style bistro is often packed for brunch on weekends.

AROUND PARLIAMENT

Buda Castle may have the benefit of its location on top of Castle Hill, but the city's defining sight remains its magnificent Parliament building, set in the northern part of Pest. Extending east from the banks of the Danube, the area around Parliament is redolent with history and power, with large squares, wide, elegant avenues and Secession architecture – remnants of the once-powerful Austro-Hungarian Empire. Several of the city's most important buildings, including the imposing St Stephen's Basilica and the outstanding Hungarian State Opera, are located here. The area is also home to some of Budapest's finest restaurants, as well as its most exclusive shops and residences.

For places to stay in this area, see p117

1 Széchenyi István Square

K3 V, Széchenyi István tér

Originally known as Unloading Square, this place was renamed Franz József Square to mark the coronation. From 1947 to 2011 it was named after US president Franklin D Roosevelt. Currently, it bears the name of the founder of the Academy of Sciences. The square features a number of fine hotels, including the Gresham Palace *(p87)*.

2 Margaret Island

Inhabited as far back as Roman times, Margaret Island *(p32)*, a tranquil oasis in the middle of the Danube, is a beautiful green space that has been open to the public since 1869. The 3-km- (2-mile-) long island served as a popular hunting ground for medieval kings, while monks were drawn to its peaceful setting. Today, it offers the perfect escape after a busy day of sightseeing in the city.

3 Hungarian Parliament

Constructed in 1902 to house the National Assembly, Hungary's Parliament building *(p22)* remains the city's primary source of civic pride. It was designed by Imre Steindl, a professor at Budapest's University of Technology and Economics, who won an open competition held to find an architect for the building. Inspired by London's Houses of Parliament, this magnificent edifice is filled with paintings, frescoes and tapestries by renowned Hungarian artists. The interior can only be seen on one of the guided tours, which take place when Parliament is not in session.

4 Kossuth Lajos Square

K1 V, Kossuth Lajos tér

Still considered the best address in the city, Budapest's finest square is surrounded on all sides by splendid buildings. It was developed at the end of the 19th century, following the unification of Buda and Pest. The square is named after Lajos Kossuth, who led the 1848–49 uprising against the Habsburgs and subsequently became a member of Hungary's first democratic government. He was exiled in 1849 after the uprising was suppressed. A monument in front of the Parliament commemorates the uprising. Opposite is another that pays tribute to Ferenc II Rákóczi, leader of the 1703 revolt against Austrian rule. The largest monument in the square, the Memorial of Unity (or Trianon Memorial) was built to mark the 100th anniversary of the Treaty of Trianon, in which Hungary lost two-thirds of its former territory.

Admiring Buda from Kossuth Lajos Square

St Stephen's Basilica overlooking Zrinyi utca

5 St Stephen's Basilica

Visible from all over the city, the dome of St Stephen's Basilica *(p26)* is exactly the same height as that of the Hungarian Parliament. Construction of the basilica began in 1851 but its completion was delayed after the original dome collapsed in 1868; it was finally completed in 1905. Today, it is one of the city's most sacred sites, as it houses the mummified right hand of St Stephen (István).

6 Academy of Sciences

K2 V, Széchenyi István tér 9 9am–4pm Mon–Fri mta.hu

Inaugurated in 1864, the Academy of Sciences is a classic piece of Neo-Renaissance architecture designed by Friedrich Stüler. Its façade is adorned with statues created by Miklós Izsó and Emil Wolff, representing the six disciplines of knowledge: mathematics, history, sciences, philosophy, law and linguistics.

SIR THOMAS GRESHAM

Although one of the city's finest buildings bears his name, Sir Thomas Gresham never set foot in Budapest. Gresham Palace was commissioned over 300 years after his death by the insurance company he had set up. The principal figure in the founding of the London Royal Exchange, Gresham is best remembered for the maxim he popularized: "bad money drives out good".

7 Liberty Square

K2 V, Szabadság tér

Laid out in 1886 on the site of the barracks that housed the Austrian army, Liberty Square has long been synonymous with Hungary's freedom struggle. The first prime minister of independent Hungary, Count Lajos Batthyány, was executed in the barracks on 6 Oct 1849. The square was also the site of the 1956 protests against the Soviet Union. Today, an eternal flame at the corner of Aulich utca and Hold utca pays tribute to Batthyány, while the statue on the northern side honours Soviet troops who liberated the city in 1944–45.

8 Hungarian State Opera

This stunning building *(p40)* is one of Europe's finest concert halls, and the best way to see it is by attending a performance. World-class operas and ballets are performed almost every evening, and tickets are very reasonably priced.

9 Operetta Theatre

M2 VI, Nagymező utca 17 By appointment only operett.hu

Operettas (one-act or light operas) have been performed here since 1898 when the building opened as the Orfeum Theatre. Designed by Viennese architects Fellner and Helmer, it was modified and renamed the Operetta Theatre in 1923, as it provided a home for the thriving operetta scene. It was further renovated in 1999–2001, but the interior remained faithful to the original design.

10 Gresham Palace

K3 V, Széchenyi István tér 5–7 24 hours daily fourseasons.com/budapest

Designed by Zsigmond Quittner and the brothers József and László Vágó in 1907, Gresham Palace is set in one of Budapest's best locations opposite the Chain Bridge. It is an imposing edifice with several Secessionist features, such as stained-glass windows (including one featuring a portrait of the patriot Lajos Kossuth), a high atrium and a chandelier. Today, it houses a Four Seasons hotel *(p117)*.

Modern glass-domed roof in the lobby of Gresham Palace

A DAY AROUND PARLIAMENT

Morning

Start with a sandwich or one of the excellent sweets at the **Szamos Today** café *(Kossuth Lajos tér 10; 06 269 02 16; open 7:30am–7pm daily)*. Then take a leisurely stroll, crossing **Kossuth Lajos Square** *(p85)* to the sensational **Hungarian Parliament** *(p22)*, where you can join one of several guided tours. After this, walk along the scenic Danube embankment to **Széchenyi István Square** *(p85)* at the head of **Chain Bridge** *(p53)*. End the morning with a light lunch on the terrace of the **Four Seasons Hotel Gresham Palace**.

Afternoon

Walk along **Zrinyi utca**, one of Budapest's foremost residential streets, famous for its smart Secessionist-style apartment buildings, to the magnificent **St Stephen's Basilica** *(p26)*. Climb the steps to the top of the church's dome for splendid views of the city. Then head to the **Hungarian State Opera** *(p40)*, timing your arrival to coincide with one of the daily guided tours at 3pm or 4pm. Eat an early dinner at **Klassz** *(p89)* and then prepare for a night at the opera (make sure you reserve tickets in advance). Afterwards, have a drink at nearby **Boutiq'Bar** *(p88)* to round off a wonderful day.

Cafés and Pubs

1. Ötkert

K2 V, Zrínyi utca 4 11pm–5am Thu–Sun othert.hu

Budapest's most popular club offers two different spaces, each with its own music and vibe depending on the DJs.

2. Cat Café

K2 Révay utca 3 10am–9pm daily catcafebudapest.hu

A must-visit spot for cat lovers, this pretty little café has plenty of felines you can make friends with between the coffee, tea, cakes and cocktails.

3. Cause Café & Roastery

L2 Zrínyi utca 12 9am–6pm daily

One of Budapest's leading gourmet coffee hubs, this spot offers a wide range of divine roasts. Don't miss its chocolate banana bread.

4. Drop Shop Wine Bar

C2 Balassi Bálint utca 27 11am–midnight daily dropshop.hu

Choose from more than 60 varieties of wine by the glass as well as a great selection of bar snacks here.

5. The Box Donut

L1 Teréz körút 62 7:42am–8:08pm daily (from 9:42am Sun) theboxdonut.com

This place serves square-shaped handmade doughnuts in 25 flavours, plus sandwiches and coffee.

6. Európa Kávéház

C2 Szent István Krt 7–9 06 1 312 23 62 7am–8pm daily

Savour pastries, cakes and choose from at least eight different kinds of hot chocolate at this classic café.

7. Boutiq'Bar

L3 VI, Paulay Ede utca 5 Hours vary, check website boutiqbar.com

Known for its excellent cocktails and friendly staff, Boutiq'Bar gets very busy after 9pm.

8. Tóth Kocsma

C2 V, Falk Miksa utca 17 06 1 302 64 42 2pm–midnight Mon–Fri, 5pm–midnight Sat

Tóth Kocsma is a must-visit if you want a pint or a *pálinka* with the locals. Try the elderflower cider.

9. AlterEgo

C3 VI, Dessewffy utca 33 10pm–5am Fri & Sat alteregoclub.hu

Budapest's leading LGBTQ+ bar and club plays classic pop hits and welcomes everyone.

10. Tokaji Borozó

C3 V, Falk Miksa utca 32 06 1 269 31 43 1–11pm Mon–Fri

This Hungarian wine bar is dedicated to the famed sweet dessert wines that are sold under the Tokaji name.

A lounging feline in Budapest's Cat Café

Restaurants

Stylish dining area at Kollázs

PRICE CATEGORIES

For a three-course meal for one, with half a bottle of wine (or equivalent meal), taxes and extra charges.

F under Ft7,500 **FF** Ft7,500–Ft12,500 **FFF** over Ft12,500

1. Kollázs

K3 V, Széchenyi István tér 5–6 6:30am–10pm daily kollazs.hu • FF

At Kollázs, you can dine on inventive European cuisine and Hungarian signature specialties.

2. Iguana

K2 V, Zoltán utca 16 11:30–12:30am daily iguana.hu • FF

Enjoy hearty portions of delectable fajitas, tortillas and burritos at reasonable prices at Iguana.

3. Ape Regina Restaurant & Bar

L1 Podmaniczky utca 18 Noon–midnight daily aperegina.hu • FF

Ape Regina is an all-you-can-eat Italian restaurant. Some drinks are also included in the fixed price.

4. Onyx Restaurant

K3 V, Vörösmarty tér 7–8 Noon–2:30pm & 6:30–11pm Tue–Fri, 6:30–11pm Sat onyxrestaurant.hu • FFF

Indulge in delectable haute cuisine without spending a fortune by selecting one of the set menus here.

5. Imázs Restaurant

L2 1065, Hajós utca 16–18 Noon–11pm daily imazsetterem.com • FF

Located in the heart of Budapest, this Asian restaurant serves great Thai and Japanese cuisine.

6. Hungarikum Bisztró

K2 Steindl Imre utca 13 Noon–2:30pm & 6–10pm daily hungarikumbisztro.hu • F

This fabulous Hungarian restaurant serves classic local dishes; be sure to book weeks in advance to get a table.

7. Sir Lancelot

C3 VI, Podmaniczky utca 14 Noon–midnight daily sirlancelot.hu • FF

This themed restaurant serves huge portions of medieval dishes, from marrow bones and pork knuckles to whole geese and chickens.

8. Klassz

M2 VI, Andrássy út 41 11:30am–11pm daily • FF

A modern bistro and café, Klassz offers international dishes, made using local ingredients, and excellent wines. Note, reservations are not accepted.

9. Kisharang Étkezde

K2 Október 6 utca 17 11:30am–10pm daily kisharang.hu • F

A fantastic little Hungarian restaurant, Kisharang Étkezde serves local comfort food at bargain prices. Check the blackboard for the daily specials.

10. Café Kör

L3 V, Sas utca 17 06 1 311 00 53 Noon–10pm Mon–Sat • FF

This café is legendary among expats, who flock here for light meals, good drinks and a great atmosphere. Note that credit cards are not accepted.

CENTRAL PEST

Known as Belváros or the Inner City, this area was a trading hub as far back as the 11th century, thanks to its riverside position. It's still the city's commercial hub, and is filled with fine buildings, shops and cafés. The area lay in ruins at the end of the 17th century, and was only redeveloped in the 19th century when a number of what are now Pest's most important buildings were built, including the Hungarian National Museum. Today, many of the streets and squares are entirely pedestrianized, making it an ideal place for walking, shopping and dining outdoors. In fact, during the summer, the southern end of Váci Street becomes a never-ending melee of cafés and pubs, with revellers drinking on the pavements from dawn to dusk.

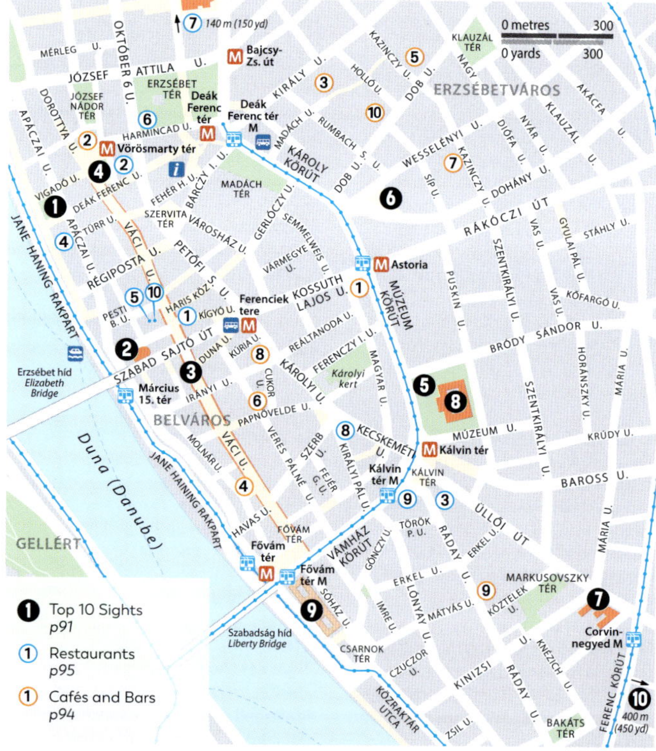

For places to stay in this area, see p118

Pedestrianized Váci Street lined with shops

1 Vigadó Square

K4 V, Vigadó tér

Facing the Danube, Vigadó Square is one of Budapest's quietest spots. It is dominated by the Vigadó Concert Hall, under whose sublime colonnades visitors seek shade during hot summer afternoons. Designed by Frigyes Feszl and built between 1859 and 1864, it replaced an earlier hall that was destroyed during the 1848–49 uprising. The façade is a wonder of arched windows, statues and busts, with an old Hungarian coat of arms in the centre. The building was badly damaged during World War II, but substantial restoration efforts faithfully returned it to its former glory. Facing the hall is the Modernist Budapest Marriott Hotel, built in 1969. Danube river cruises *(p52)* depart from the jetties on the square's embankment.

2 Inner City Parish Church

K4 V, Március 15 tér 2

061 318 31 08 9am–7pm daily

Pest's oldest church has a long and varied history. The original Romanesque structure, erected in 1046 by Hungary's first king St Stephen (István) on the burial site of the martyred St Gellért, was decimated by the Tartars, and its 14th-century replacement was converted into a mosque by the Turks. It was nearly destroyed again after World War II, when builders wanted to demolish it to make way for the Elizabeth Bridge *(p52)*, but luckily, it was saved at the last minute. The church hosts free organ concerts, plus a number of sacred and classical music performances.

3 Váci Street

One of Pest's oldest streets, Váci Street *(p28)* originally led to the town of Vác *(p69)*. As Pest prospered, so did the street, and it soon became a favourite among Budapest's wealthy citizens. The goods stores gave way to exclusive boutiques, and today it is one of the city's most popular shopping venues. The northern half is dominated by retail outlets and department stores. The pedestrianized southern end of Váci Street is home to some of the area's best cafés and clubs. The street has become increasingly touristy in recent decades, but has nevertheless retained its eclectic feel.

4 Vörösmarty Square

K3 V, Vörösmarty tér

This splendid pedestrian plaza is named after the poet Mihály Vörösmarty, whose statue stands at its centre. Designed by the sculptor Ede Telcs and made of Carrara marble, the statue rallies the nation in the poet's own words: "Your homeland, Hungary, serve unwaveringly." The northern side of the square is dominated by Gerbeaud Cukrászda *(p94)*, one of Hungary's most famous coffee houses, opened by pastry chef Henrik Kugler in 1858. It is also worth visiting the quaint metro station.

JEWISH QUARTER

Budapest's Jewish Quarter is based just north of Károly körút. The community thrived here until 1941, when anti-Semitic laws were passed by the government of Admiral Horthy. By 1944 much of the area was a ghetto, and thousands had been deported to death camps. Today the community is thriving once again, with synagogues, shops and kosher restaurants.

5 Mihály Pollack Square

D5 V, Pollach Mihály tér

Named after the architect of several Neo-Classical buildings in the city, this square is famous for its three palaces – Count Károlyi at No 6, Prince Eszterházy at No 8 and Prince Festetics at No 10. The superb façades of the palaces (only Festetics Palace is open to the public), make this square one of the most picturesque in the city.

6 Great Synagogue

Built in Byzantine style by Viennese architect Ludwig Förster in 1854–49, the largest synagogue *(p44)* in Europe can hold over 3,000 people. It houses the Hungarian Jewish Museum *(p50)*, which chronicles the long history of the city's Jewish people. At the rear of the synagogue is the Raoul Wallenberg Memorial Park, which features the *Tree of Life*, a Holocaust memorial. Designed by Imre Varga, each leaf of this silver weeping willow tree bears the name of one of the 600,000 Hungarian Jewish people killed during the Holocaust.

7 Museum of Applied Arts

D5 IX, Üllői út 33–7 For renovation imm.hu

The opening of this museum was the finale of the city's 1896 Millennium Celebrations *(p98)*. Created to house the Hungarian State's sizeable collection of art, the exquisite building was designed by Ödön Lechner and Gyula Pártos. Like many Secessionist buildings, it incorporates elements inspired by Asian art and architecture, such as a green dome and a glass-roofed courtyard. The museum exhibits works of fine arts and crafts as well as traditional costumes.

8 Hungarian National Museum

A treasure-trove of art and artifacts, the Hungarian National Museum *(p42)* was founded by Count Ferenc Széchényi, who donated his extensive collections of books and art to the nation. Designed by Mihály Pollack, the building's steps are notable as the site where Sándor

Artifact in the Hungarian National Museum

Petofi recited his poem *Nemzeti Dal* (National Song), which sparked the uprising of 1848–49. This historic event is commemorated every year with a reenactment on 15 March.

9 Corvinus University of Budapest

L6 V, Fővám tér 8
uni-corvinus.hu

A Neo-Renaissance masterpiece, this university was built between 1871 and 1874 to house the city's main customs house. Designed by Miklós Ybl, its Danube façade is set on three levels – a colonnade supporting a balcony, with two rows of arched windows facing the river. The balustrade supports 10 allegorical figures sculpted by August Sommer. The building became the University of Economics in 1951, when it was named after Karl Marx. It was given its current name in 2000.

10 Holocaust Memorial Center

E6 IX, Páva utca 39 10am–6pm Tue–Sun hdke.hu

This centre was founded both in order to collect and study material relating to the history of the Holocaust and to honour its victims. A permanent exhibition examines the persecution and suffering of Hungary's Jewish and Roma communities during the Holocaust, with special focus on the relationship between the state and its citizens. The centre also contains a Wall of Remembrance on which the name of every Hungarian victim of the Holocaust will one day be engraved. There's also a restored synagogue, dating from 1924, which now hosts temporary exhibitions.

Geometric interior of the Great Synagogue

A DAY IN DOWNTOWN BUDAPEST

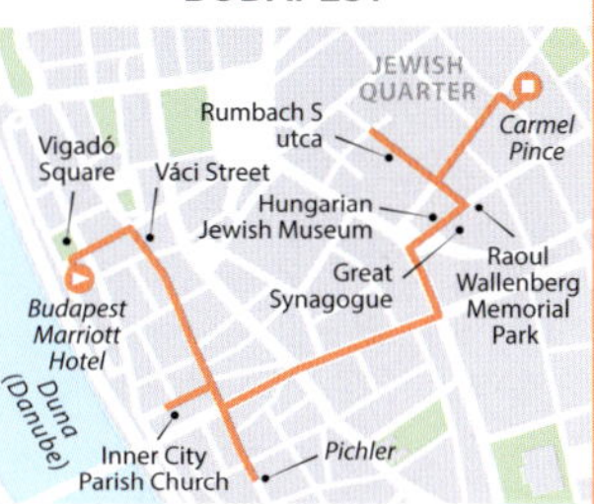

Morning

A leisurely cup of coffee on the terrace of the Modernist **Budapest Marriott Hotel** on Vigadó Square will set the tone for the day. Then walk a short distance east to **Váci Street** *(p28)*, with its plethora of retail stores and cafés. Next, visit Pest's oldest church, the **Inner City Parish Church** *(p91)* just off Szabad Sajtó út, before stopping for a sweet Hungarian Chimney Cake at **Pichler** *(pichlerbudapest.com)*.

Afternoon

After lunch, either take the metro from Ferenciek tere up to Astoria or walk ten minutes along the busy Kossuth Lajos utca to the **Great Synagogue** on Dohány utca. Visit the Byzantine-inspired synagogue and its excellent **Hungarian Jewish Museum** *(p50)* before paying your respects to the Jewish people killed in the Holocaust at the sobering *Tree of Life* memorial in the **Raoul Wallenberg Memorial Park**, located in the courtyard at the back of the synagogue. Then explore the rest of the **Jewish Quarter**, known for its little gift shops and quaint book stores, as well as the far less ostentatious synagogues on **Rumbach S utca** and Kazinczy utca. End your day with a delicious glatt-kosher dinner at the **Carmel Pince** restaurant *(Kazinczy utca 31)*.

Cafés and Bars

Szimpla Kert, Budapest's original ruin bar

1. Café Astoria

M4 V, Kossuth Lajos utca 19–21 7am–10pm daily cafeastoria budapest.hu

An elegant café inside Hotel Astoria that manages to turn even a cup of coffee into an event.

2. Gerbeaud Cukrászda

K3 V, Vörösmarty tér 7 9am–8pm daily (to 9pm Fri & Sat) gerbeaud.hu

Beautifully decorated cakes complement the grand old-world interiors of the city's oldest and finest café.

3. Spíler BistroPub

M3 Király utca 13, Gozsdu udvar 11:30–1:30am daily spilerbp.hu

Spíler comprises two venues – Spíler Classic is a gastropub, while Spíler Shanghai is more like a speakeasy.

4. 1000 Tea

L5 V, Váci utca 65 Noon–9pm Mon–Sat 1000tea.hu

This café offers a variety of teas and a soundtrack of soothing music, making it the perfect spot to unwind.

5. Kőleves (Stonesoup)

M3 VII, Kazinczy utca 37–41 Noon–10pm daily (to 11pm Thu-Sat) kolevesvendeglo.hu

Surrounded by mulberry trees, this laidback bar's pebbled courtyard, with colourful chairs and even a hammock, is very popular with families.

6. Good Spirit Bar

C5 V, Veres Pálné u. 7 3pm–midnight daily (to 1am Fri & Sat) goodspiritbar.hu

This popular bar promises a huge array of whiskies, bottled beers and cocktails, all of which are served alongside tasty snacks.

7. Szimpla Kert

M3 VII, Kazinczy utca 14 3pm–4am daily (from noon Fri & Sat, 9am Sun) szimpla.hu

Housed in a refurbished apartment block, Szimpla Kert is the biggest ruined-garden bar in the seventh district.

8. Centrál Grand Cafe & Bar

M5 Károlyi utca 9 9am–midnight Wed–Sat, 9am–10pm Sun–Tue centralgrandcafe.hu

Opened in 1887, this café is known for its Art Nouveau style and excellent coffee, tea, cakes and cocktails, not to mention the city's finest crêpes.

9. Paris, Texas

D5 IX, Ráday utca 22 06 1 218 05 70 5pm–4am daily

A late-night hotspot for those who like to stop for a nightcap on their way home. The Texan link is reinforced by the range of malt whiskies on offer.

10. Doblo

M3 VII, Dob utca 20 5pm–1am Wed & Thu, 5pm–2am Fri & Sat doblo.hu

Sample wines from all over the world at this elegant bar, located in the heart of downtown Pest.

Restaurants

1. Apostolok

L4 V, Kígyó utca 4–6 8am–11pm daily apostoloketterem.hu • FFF

Originally established as a pub in 1902, this centrally located restaurant offers traditional Hungarian flavours.

2. Vapiano

C4 V, Vörösmarty tér 3 11am–11pm daily (to 9pm Sun) vapiano.hu • FFF

Enjoy fabulous views of Vörösmarty Square while tucking into delicious Italian food.

3. Costes

M5 IX, Ráday utca 4 6–11pm Wed–Sun costes.hu • FFF

White-gloved waiters glide from table to table at this chic restaurant, the first in the city to earn a Michelin star.

4. DNB Restaurant

C4 V, Duna korzó (Marriott Hotel) 6:30am–11pm daily dnbbudapest.com • FFF

Adopting a farm-to-table concept, this spot serves delicious, seasonal dishes made with locally sourced ingredients.

5. Babel

L4 V, Piarista köz 2 5:30pm–midnight Tue–Sat babel-budapest.hu • FFF

At the foot of the Elizabeth Bridge, this bistro offers attentive service and food made with fresh ingredients.

Brick-walled industrial decor of Kiosk

PRICE CATEGORIES

For a three-course meal for one, with half a bottle of wine (or equivalent meal), taxes and extra charges.

F under Ft7,500 **FF** Ft7,500–Ft12,500 **FFF** over Ft12,500

6. Nobu

K3 V, Kempinski Hotel Corvinus, Erzsébet tér 7–8 Noon–11pm daily (to 11:45pm Fri & Sat) noburestaurants.com • FFF

Known for its delectable sushi and other Japanese delicacies, luxurious Nobu attracts an elite crowd.

7. Comme Chez Soi

K4 V, Aranykéz utca 2 Noon–11pm Tue–Sat commechezsoi.hu • FFF

Fine Italian cuisine makes up the menu at this charming little place. You will need to reserve a table a day or two in advance, but its worth the admin.

8. Salt

M5 Királyi Pál utca 4 6–11pm Wed–Sun saltbudapest.com • FFF

Salt's signature 14-dish tasting menu, featuring locally sourced ingredients, is an exquisite, if expensive, treat.

9. Pata Negra

M5 Kalvin ter 8 11am–11pm daily patanegra.hu • FF

Choose from a wide range of tapas and Spanish dishes, as well as Budapest's best selection of Spanish wines.

10. Kiosk Budapest

L4 V, Március 15 tér 4 1–11pm daily (to midnight Fri & Sat) kiosk-budapest.hu • FFF

Once a warehouse, this vast space has been converted into a trendy bar and restaurant serving simple but beautifully presented food, including one of the best burgers in the city.

AROUND CITY PARK

Home to some of the finest buildings and widest boulevards in the city, the area around City Park (Városliget) is a favourite local spot. In 1896, it was chosen as the central location for Budapest's Millennium Celebrations, commemorating the 1,000-year anniversary of the Magyars' conquest of the Carpathian Basin. Everything here is built on a grand scale, from the cafés of Liszt Ferenc tér to the mansions of Andrássy út and Városligeti Terrace. Even the City Park itself – fronted by the Millennium Monument – features two museums, the House of Music and the Hungarian Ethnographic Museum, and the fairy-tale Vajdahunyad Castle as attractions. Beyond the park, you'll find the Museum of Fine Arts and iconic Heroes' Square. In 1879, a hot spring was discovered at the park's edge, leading to the opening of the Széchenyi Baths at the same site just over three decades later.

For places to stay in this area, see p118

Raphael's *Portrait of Pietro Bembo* (c 1504), Museum of Fine Arts

1 Museum of Fine Arts

E2 XIV, Hősök tere, Dózsa György út 41 10am–6pm Tue–Sun szepmuveszeti.hu

Hungary's largest collection of international art is housed in a 1906 building designed by Fülöp Herzog and Albert Schikendanz. It has works by Raphael, Goya, Velázquez and El Greco.

2 Andrássy Avenue

L2, M2

A long, wide boulevard stretching from City Park to the city centre, Andrássy Avenue, or Andrássy út, is Budapest's most exclusive address. It is lined with restaurants, theatres and shops, as well as the State Opera *(p40)*. At No 22 is the Drechsler Palace, built by the Hungarian Railways as rental apartments for its pension fund in 1883 and later used as the Hungarian Ballet Academy. The building is presently empty, but there are plans to turn it into a luxury hotel. The House of Terror Museum *(p98)* is further down the street, at No 60. Under Andrássy út runs Metro 1, Hungary's oldest – and the world's second-oldest – underground railway. It was declared a UNESCO World Heritage Site in 2002.

3 House of Music

The futuristic-looking House of Music *(p30)* features concert halls, an open-air stage and a permanent exhibition that offers a fascinating audio and visual tour through the history of music.

4 Széchenyi Baths

F2 XIV, Állatkerti út 11 Thermal pool: 6am–7pm daily; swimming pool and steam rooms: 6am–10pm daily szechenyibath.com

Opened in 1913, Széchenyi is a vast complex of pools, including Hungary's deepest and hottest thermal baths. In the many steaming pools, the water reaches reaches the surface at a steamy 74° C (165° F). There's also an adventure pool that features its own whirlpool.

Relaxing in the outdoor pool at Széchenyi Baths

Vajdahunyad Castle overlooking City Park's lake

5 Heroes' Square

E2 Hősök tere

Laid out in the 1890s, Heroes' Square was the focal point of Hungary's Millennium Celebrations in 1896. At its heart is the 36-m (110-ft) Millennium Monument, flanked by two colonnades. The riders on horseback at the foot of the monument represent the chieftains of the seven Magyar tribes that settled in Hungary.

6 Franz Liszt Museum

D3 VI, Vörösmarty utca 35 10am–6pm Mon–Fri, 9am–5pm Sat lisztmuseum.hu

Better known by his Germanic name Franz, Ferenc Liszt was Hungary's greatest composer. He lived here from 1881 until his death in 1886. The house became a museum in 1986, and the furniture, pianos and manuscripts exhibited here provide an insight into the life and work of this musical genius.

7 Műcsarnok (Kunsthalle)

E2 XIV, Hősök tere 10am–6pm Tue, Wed & Fri–Sun; noon–8pm Thu mucsarnok.hu

Situated opposite the Museum of Fine Arts, the Műcsarnok (literally "art hall") was completed in 1895. The imposing building, dominated by its portico with six supporting columns, was designed by Fülöp Herzog and Albert Schikendanz. Today, it hosts temporary exhibitions and concerts.

8 House of Terror Museum

D3 VI, Andrássy út 60 10am–6pm Tue–Sun terrorhaza.hu

This building was the headquarters of the Fascist Arrow Cross party before and during World War II, and later for the secret police. Exhibits include a T54 tank used in the repression of the 1956 revolution. The basement, which was a prison during both regimes, has a recreated cell that looks just like it did in the 1940s.

THE MILLENNIUM EXHIBITION

Much of City Park was built for the 1896 Millennium Exhibition, which celebrated 1,000 years since the Magyars first inhabited the area near Budapest. The exhibition also saw the opening of the millennium metro line – continental Europe's first – the installation of the city's first gas lights and the construction of a number of Secessionist buildings.

9 Vajdahunyad Castle

F2 Vajdahunyad sétány

Located in the heart of City Park, Vajdahunyad Castle was designed by Hungarian architect Ignác Alpár for the Millennium Celebrations. Alpár's design aimed to showcase the entire evolution of Hungarian architecture in a single structure. To achieve this, each section of the castle reflects important edifices from the Renaissance, Gothic, Baroque and Romanesque styles – the complex represents over 20 famous Hungarian buildings. The Museum of Agriculture *(mezogazdasagimuzeum.hu)* in the Baroque section is the only part of the castle open to the public.

10 Hungarian Ethnographic Museum

E2 Dózsa György út 35 10am–6pm Tue–Sun (to 8pm Thu & Sat) neprajz.hu

Opened in 2022, the Hungarian Ethnographic Museum in Heroes' Square showcases the rich cultural heritage of Central Europe. Described by its designers as a "landscraper", approximately 60 per cent of the building is situated underground to avoid overshadowing City Park. An architectural masterpiece, the museum has an extensive collection of old photographs, furniture, costumes and tools that depict Hungarian life from the end of the 18th century until World War I. A 24-hour roof garden atop the building offers stunning city views.

A DAY IN CITY PARK

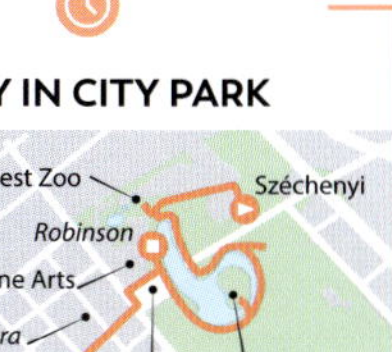

Morning

Start off early with a dip in Budapest's most popular thermal baths, **Széchenyi** *(p97)*, situated right in the middle of City Park with its own metro station on the Lilliputian Millennium line. Refreshed, head over next door to the **Budapest Zoo** *(p58)*. You can get information about the programmes for the day at the entrance. Then, take a walk around the park's lake at Kós Károly sétány. Follow it up with fresh coffee and delectable sandwiches at the Turkish coffee house **Café Kara** *(p100)* on Andrássy Avenue.

Afternoon

The first stop in the afternoon is the **Museum of Fine Arts** *(p97)* in **Heroes' Square**. Although you could spend all afternoon here, try to restrict yourself to an hour and a half, but be sure not to miss Raphael's *Madonna* or the collection of El Grecos. Next up is a ride on the historic M1 metro line between Heroes' Square and the **Oktogon**. Afterwards, head back to the park to admire the architecture of **Vajdahunyad Castle**, ideally from a rowing boat on the park's central lake. If you are visiting in winter, you can go ice-skating on the lake *(p59)*. End the day with a delicious dinner at **Robinson** *(p101)*, one of Budapest's most famous restaurants.

Art Deco-style interior of the New York Café és Étterem

Cafés and Pubs

1. New York Café és Étterem

D4 VII, Erzsébet körút 9–11 8am–10pm daily newyorkcafe.hu

Sip hot chocolate or a martini at this lavish Budapest institution, once a meeting spot for the city's literati.

2. A99

E2 Andrássy út 99 70 8:30am–5:30pm Mon–Sat

Enjoy excellent coffee and people-watching at A99 – one of the city's best spots for coffee lovers.

3. Kaledonia

M1 VI, Mozsár utca 9 2pm–midnight daily (from noon Sat & Sun) kaledoniabudapest.hu

This Scottish pub is the perfect spot for watching sporting events and enjoying hearty meals.

4. Menza

M2 VI, Liszt Ferenc tér 2 11am–11pm daily menzaetterem.hu

Menza's restaurant and coffee house offers a modern take on Magyar canteen favorites, all in a retro-inspired setting.

5. Café Vian

M2 VI, Liszt Ferenc tér 9 9am–1am daily cafevian.com

Coffee, cocktails, pasta and salads along with traditional Hungarian fare make Vian a one-stop shop.

6. Sugar Shop

M2 Paulay Ede utca 48 11am–7pm daily sugarshop.hu

Sample irresistible, colourful sweets at this lovely confectionery and candy shop.

7. Unity Bar & Brewery

E3 Király utca 101 Hours vary, check website unitybrewing.hu

The selection of craft beers on offer here changes regularly, but always includes a mix of lagers, IPAs and dark beers.

8. Flow

D3 VI, Andrássy út 66 9am–6pm daily flowcoffee.hu

Come here for coffee and tea from around the world, and a menu that is a treat for vegans and vegetarians.

9. Café Kara

E2 VI, Andrássy út 130 10am–10pm daily cafekara.hu

A dog-friendly, Turkish-style coffee and beer house, Café Kara offers a range of cocktails, too.

10. Két Szerecsen

D3 Nagymező utca 14 8:30am–11:30pm daily (from 9am Sat & Sun) ketszerecsen.hu

This Parisian bistro has good-value, tasty food and coffee, plus an extensive wine menu.

Restaurants

1. Gundel

E2 Gundel Károly út 4 11:30am–10pm daily (to 4pm Sun) gundel.hu • FFF

Probably Hungary's most famous restaurant and one of the priciest, Gundel serves traditional yet creative food.

2. Parázs Presszo Thai Restaurant

D3 Jókai utca 8 Noon–10pm daily parazspresszo.com • FF

Known for its spicy Thai food, this small restaurant also has good vegan, vegetarian and gluten-free options.

3. Porto di Pest

M2 VI, Liszt Ferenc tér 3 06 1 351 87 38 11am–1am daily • FF

A popular spot that attracts more locals than tourists, Porto di Pest serves delicious goulash, burgers and local beers.

4. Maharaja

D3 VII, Csengery utca 24 Noon–11pm daily maharaja.hu • FF

Family-run Maharaja presents subtly spiced, mouthwatering curries from the Indian subcontinent.

5. Trattoria Gusto

M2 VI, Liszt Ferenc tér 11 Noon–11pm daily (to midnight Fri & Sat) • FF

Delectable clay-oven pizzas and other Italian delicacies are served in a pretty dining room.

6. Arriba Taqueria

D3 VI, Teréz körút 25 11am–10pm daily arriba.hu • F

Although essentially just fast food served at the counter, this is the best Tex-Mex restaurant in Budapest.

7. The Big Fish

D3 VI, Andrássy út 44 Noon–10pm daily thebigfish.hu • FFF

At The Big Fish, you can pick what you like from the fresh seafood counter and have it cooked just the way you like it.

PRICE CATEGORIES

For a three-course meal for one, with half a bottle of wine (or equivalent meal), taxes and extra charges.

F under Ft7,500 **FF** Ft7,500–Ft12,500 **FFF** over Ft12,500

8. Király100

D3 VI, Király utca 100 11:30am–10:30pm daily (to 11pm Fri & Sat) kiraly100.hu • FFF

This bistro serves amazing steaks, and offers a vast selection of *pálinka* (Hungarian fruit brandy, p61).

9. Alice

E2 Andrássy út 116 Noon–9:30pm daily alicehotel.hu • F

One of the best value-for-money places to eat and drink on all of Andrássy út, Alice serves simple, delicious meals on a leafy terrace.

10. Robinson

E2 XIV, Városligeti-tó Noon–4pm & 6–11pm daily robinsonrestaurant.hu • FF

This casual seafood restaurant is located on a charming island in the middle of Városliget lake.

Busy fresh seafood counter at The Big Fish

GREATER BUDAPEST

While the city centre has enough to keep most visitors happy for weeks, Budapest's suburbs spread out into the surrounding Pannonian plains and feature some extraordinary sights, many dating back to the Roman era. These include the former Roman city of Aquincum, nestled on the banks of the Danube and once home to a sizable amphitheatre. Today, the site is bordered by a train line and a highway. To the southwest is the former Roman garrison at Óbuda, where ancient aqueducts, baths and barracks have been carefully excavated. The Buda Hills, once some distance from the city, now have villas and apartment blocks extending into their foothills; from here, the narrow-gauge Children's Railway is a popular means of exploring the region. The area is home to natural wonders, too, with the remarkable limestone caves at Pálvölgy and Szemlő-hegyi offering a fascinating glimpse into Budapest's unique geology.

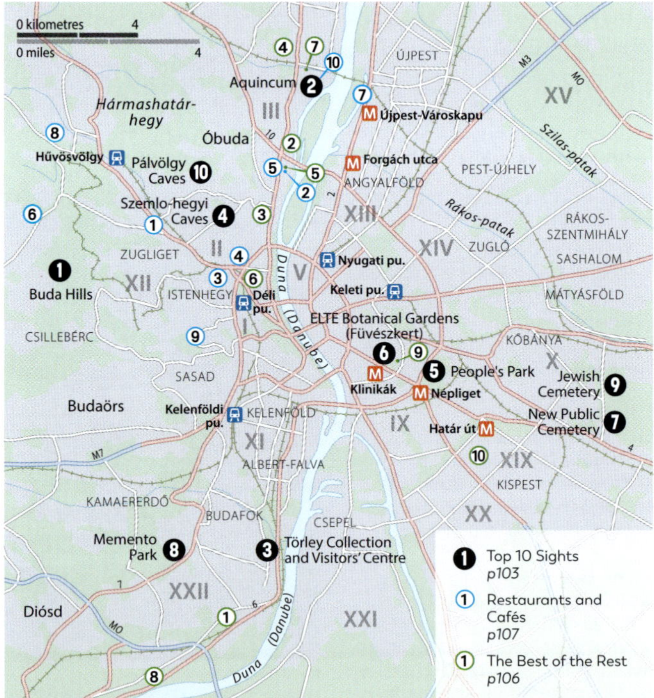

For places to stay in this area, see p119

Elizabeth Lookout Tower atop János Hill

1 Buda Hills

N1

Located just west of the city, the forested Buda Hills are a popular getaway for city locals. The best way to reach the area is to hop on the Cogwheel Railway, which departs from Városmajor. Once in the countryside, visitors can walk leafy trails, hike to the Elizabeth Lookout Tower (which offers stunning views of the city) or hop on the Children's Railway *(p59)*, which meanders through the Buda Hills towards Huvös Valley.

2 Aquincum

P1 III, Szentendrei út 139
Apr–Oct: 9am–6pm Tue–Sun; Nov–Mar: 10am–4pm Tue–Sun
aquincum.hu

The capital of the Roman province of Pannonia, Aquincum was for centuries the largest city in Central Europe. The site was excavated only at the end of the 19th century; the outlines of streets and buildings are clearly visible. The museum, inside a Neo-Classical lapidarium, houses Roman artifacts found at the site and models showing what the town once looked like.

3 Törley Collection and Visitors' Centre

P3 XXII, Anna utca 5–7 By appointment only torleymuzeum.hu

Widely recognized as the father of the Hungarian wine industry, József Törley studied wine-making in Reims, the champagne capital of France. He returned to Hungary in the 1880s and set about producing superb sparkling wine in Budafok. The Törley Collection displays the long history of Törley sparkling wines, while the centre's architecture, featuring Ottoman influences, is also a major highlight.

4 Szemlő-hegyi Caves

N1 II, Pusztaszeri út 35
10am–4pm Tue–Sun 23 Dec–1 Jan dunaipoly.hu

North of the city centre are the Pilis Hills, home to several fabulous cave systems. The Szemlő-hegyi Caves are the closest to the city and feature unique formations, known as cave pearls, that resemble grapes growing out of the rock. These are produced by the hot springs penetrating limestone. The air here is said to be therapeutic for bronchial infections.

Exploring the impressive Szemlő-hegyi Caves

IMRE NAGY

Born in 1896 to a peasant family, Imre Nagy was a hardline Communist for much of his life. During the 1956 Revolution, he became the prime minister of the Hungarian People's Republic, however, a few days later, the Soviet Union invaded Hungary and crushed the revolution. Nagy was arrested, executed and then buried in an unmarked grave.

5 People's Park

P2 VIII, Népliget

The city's largest park, Népliget, or People's Park, was laid out in the 1860s and covers an area of 112 ha (277 acres). It has large tracts of grass and trees, as well as flower beds and playgrounds. Népliget was also the site of the city's first motor racing track, and even hosted a Grand Prix in 1936. However, the track fell into disuse after a few decades.

6 ELTE Botanical Garden (Füvészkert)

F6 VIII, Illés utca 25 Apr–Oct: 10am–5pm daily; Nov–Mar: 9am–4pm daily fuveszkert.org

Spread over 3 ha (8 acres) in eastern Budapest, the ELTE Botanical Garden offers relief from the bustle of the city centre. The gardens are part of ELTE University, though they were first laid out by the Festetics family, who lived in the Neo-Classical villa that is now the administration centre. Highlights include a collection of tropical plants in the palm house.

7 New Public Cemetery

Q2 X, Kozma utca 8–10 06 30 372 28 47 Hours vary, call ahead

This peaceful cemetery, found to the southwest of Pest, is one of the largest in Europe. An expansive burial site, it is the resting place of around 1.5 million Hungarians, including former prime minister Imre Nagy and other participants of the 1956 revolution. Their graves can be found in plots 300 and 301. Nearby, there's a visitors' centre which shows a series of short films chronicling the lives of some of the people buried here.

8 Memento Park

N3 XXII, Balatoni út 10am–6pm daily mementopark.hu

The grounds of Memento Park bring together over 40 examples of the Communist-era statues and placques (some astonishingly huge) that once stood in public spaces all over Budapest. Marx, Engels and Lenin are all present, as is the Stalin pedestal, complete with a full-scale replica of his boots: these were all that remained when Stalin's statue was toppled and

Kiss István's Worker's Movement Memorial in Memento Park

destroyed during the 1956 revolution. There's also a Trabant – known as "the people's car" – on show, while multimedia displays in a barracks-style building reveal some of the methods the AVH, the Hungarian secret police, used to spy on their own people.

9 Jewish Cemetery

Q2 XVII, Kozma utca
8am–3pm Sun–Fri (summer: to 4pm)
budapestjewishcemetery.com

Opened in 1893 and full of elaborate tombs, this cemetery is a stark reminder of the wealth and influence wielded by Budapest's Jewish people before World War II. Some of the tombs were designed by leading architects, including Ödön Lechner and Gyula Fodor.

10 Pálvölgy Caves

N1 II, Szépvölgyi út 162
dunaipoly.hu

A hut at the foot of a steep cliff marks the entrance to the Pálvölgy Caves. As well as the cave "pearls" that are also found in Szemlő-hegyi, Pálvölgy is known for its formations that resemble animals. Though many of the caves are accessible, and can be visited via stairs, several of the more spectacular formations can only be seen by joining a guided tour. Remember to wear warm clothes as the temperatures inside can be chilly.

Stone statue at the ELTE Botanical Garden (Füvészkert)

A DAY IN THE BUDA HILLS

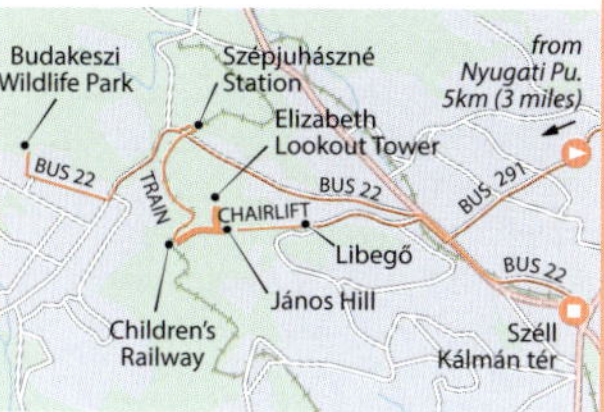

Morning

Start the day by taking bus No 291 from Nyugati Pu to its terminus at the foot of the **Libegő** (chairlift), which takes you up to the summit of **János Hill**. From here, walk to the **Children's Railway** *(p59)*, a relic of Hungary's Communist past. As the train meanders through the hills, you can stop off and climb to the top of the **Elizabeth Lookout Tower** for sensational views of the city below. Then take the steam train, which leaves on the hour throughout summer. Get off at **Szépjuhászné Station** and try the station's excellent outdoor café for lunch.

Afternoon

Set off on a well-marked path to the **Budakeszi Wildlife Park** *(vadaspark-budakeszi.hu)*. Occupying an area of 327 ha (808 acres), it's home to a wide variety of animals, from wild boars – which also roam freely in the surrounding countryside – to packs of wolves. There is also a separate reserve for plant life. Take the park's walking safari tour and enjoy climbing in the adventure park. The park's restaurant is a great place for dinner, with lively folk music and dancing every evening after 6pm. As the Children's Railway will likely be closed by the time you finish your meal, take bus No 22 to **Széll Kálmán tér**, and from there, get the metro back to the city centre.

The Best of the Rest

1. Tropicarium-Oceanarium

N3 XXII, Nagytétényí út 37–43 10am–8pm daily tropicarium.hu

Stare into the eyes of a shark or glimpse an alligator at this aquarium and indoor tropical rainforest.

2. Kassák Museum

P1 III, Fő tér 1 10am–5pm Wed–Sun kassakmuzeum.hu

Housed in Zichy Palace, this museum beautifully showcases the works of avant-garde artist Lajos Kassák.

3. Óbuda Amphitheatre

N1 III, Bécsi út

Dating from around 140–150 CE, this military amphitheatre is the larger of Budapest's two Roman amphitheatres. It still features two arched entrances and tunnels, which were originally used for the entry of wild animals.

4. Aquincum Amphitheatre

P1 III, Szentendrei út

Located between the HÉV railway and a main road is Aquincum's civil amphitheatre. It was built around 250–300 CE, with capacity for approximately 10,000 spectators.

5. Hungarian Museum of Trade and Tourism

P1 III, Korona tér 1 10am–6pm Tue–Sun mkvm.hu

Explore the rich history of Hungarian catering and home cuisine at this unique gastronomy museum. Its collection also showcases the city's trading past.

6. Hospital in the Rock Nuclear Bunker Museum

N2 I, Lovas út 4/c 10am–7pm daily sziklakorhaz.eu

Wax figures bring to life the eerie history of the system of caverns under Buda Castle, which served as an emergency hospital and shelter during World War II and became a nuclear bunker by 1962.

Well-preserved ruins of Óbuda Amphitheatre

7. Aqueduct

P1 III, Szentendrei út

A restored section of the 2nd-century aqueduct that carried water from Óbuda to Aquincum lies to the east of Szentendrei út. Traffic runs along either side, so take care.

8. Nagytétény Palace Museum

N3 XXII, Kastélypark utca 9–11 For renovation nagytetenyi.hu

Housed in one of Hungary's finest Baroque palaces, this interior design museum showcases classic furniture along with functional daily-use items.

9. Ludovika Academy

P2 X, Ludovika tér 2–6 9am–5pm Tue–Mon nhmus.hu

Once a military school, Ludovika Academy is now home to the Natural History Museum.

10. Wekerle Estate

P2 XIX, Kós Károly tér

Central Europe's first garden city, Wekerle Estate was inspired by Transylvania's Saxon villages. Built between 1909 and 1926, the houses here are much sought after.

Restaurants and Cafés

1. Remiz

N1 II, Budakeszi út 5 Noon–11pm Tue–Sat, noon–5pm Sun remiz.hu • FFF

Visit Remiz for good Hungarian food and wine, plus Budapest's best rack of ribs. There's also a lovely garden.

2. Kéhli

P1 III, Mókus utca 22 Noon–10pm daily (to 10:30pm Sat, 9pm Sun) kehli.hu • FF

Founded in 1899, Kéhli offers good, old-fashioned Hungarian food and features a live folk band on most nights.

3. Fióka

N2 XII, Városmajor utca 75 11am–11pm daily fiokaetterem.hu • FF

This charming gastropub serves a wide variety of small plates, along with a good selection of local wines.

4. Auguszt 1870 Patisserie

A3 II, Fény u. 8 10am–6pm Tue–Sat auguszt1870.hu • FFF

A local favourite, this patisserie has been serving traditional Hungarian and French-inspired pastries since 1870.

5. Zöld Kapu Vendéglő

P1 III, Szőlő utca 42 10am–11:30pm daily zoldkapuvendeglo.hu • FF

Situated in the heart of Óbuda, this spot has a pretty garden and offers hearty portions of classic Hungarian fare.

6. Budai Gesztenyés

N2 Budakeszi, Fő utca 1 11:30am–9:30pm daily (to 8pm Sun) budaigesztenyes.hu • FF

Famous for its high quality and affordable prices, this spot has a limited menu of modern European dishes with a Hungarian twist.

Elegant interior of Budai Gesztenyés

PRICE CATEGORIES

For a three-course meal for one, with half a bottle of wine (or equivalent meal), taxes and extra charges.

F under Ft7,500 **FF** Ft7,500–Ft12,500 **FFF** over Ft12,500

7. Központ Bisztró

P1 IV, Szent István tér 1 8am–10pm Mon–Fri daily (from 10am Sat & Sun) kozpontbisztro.hu • F

Open since 2013, Központ Bisztró has been popular with locals for its burgers and international cuisine.

8. Náncsi Néni

N1 II, Ördögárok út 80 Noon–10pm daily nancsineni.hu • F

Savour fantastic regional dishes made with farm-fresh ingredients in a 17th-century farmhouse.

9. Jardinette

N2 XII, Németvölgyi út 136 Noon–10pm Tue–Sat, noon–9pm Sun jardinette.hu • FF

Enjoy exquisite French food in a lovely glass-covered garden at Jardinette. The wine list is superb, too.

10. Planteen

P1 Záhony utca 7 8am–5pm Mon–Fri planteen.hu • FF

The country's first plant-based canteen and café, Planteen is known for its vegan lunches, delicious coffee and snacks.

STREETSMART

A tram crossing the Danube

48

GETTING AROUND

Whether exploring Budapest by foot or making use of public transport, here is everything you need to know to navigate the city and areas beyond the centre like a pro.

AT A GLANCE

PUBLIC TRANSPORT COSTS

SINGLE JOURNEY
450 Ft
With transfers on bus/tram/metro, up to 80 mins.

24-HOUR PASS
2,500 Ft
Unlimited travel within Budapest.

72-HOUR PASS
5,500 Ft
Unlimited travel within Budapest.

SPEED LIMIT

MOTORWAY
130 km/h (80mph)

EXPRESSWAYS
110 km/h (70mph)

RURAL ROADS
90 km/h (50mph)

URBAN AREAS
50 km/h (30mph)

Arriving by Air

All flights to Budapest arrive at **Ferenc Liszt International Airport**. It has connections to the UK and most other major European cities, as well as trans-atlantic flights to New York.

Bus line 100E serves Deák Ferenc tér in the city centre, alternatively 200E operates between Terminal 2 and Budapest's Nagyvárad tér and Népliget metro stations 24 hours a day. The bus also stops at Ferihegy vasútállomás, the airport's train station. Taxis can be ordered at **Főtaxi** booths located at the exits. **MiniBud** offers a minibus service to major hotels for a flat fee.

Ferenc Liszt International Airport
W bud.hu
Főtaxi
W fotaxi.hu
MiniBud
W minibud.hu

Train Travel

The city's main train station, Keleti, is close to the centre and served by direct trains from most major central European cities. You can buy tickets and passes for multiple international journeys via **Eurail** or **Interrail**. All trains within Hungary are run by **MÁV** (Magyar llamvasutak). Fast InterCity services within Hungary link the capital with Debrecen, Szeged, Pécs and Győr, stopping only at major towns and cities. There are a number of other services, but they are slower. Tickets can be bought at stations or online from MÁV.

Eurail
W eurail.com
Interrail
W interrail.eu
MÁV
W mav-start.hu

Public Transport

Budapest has an extensive public transport network made up of bus, trolleybus, tram and metro services.

All services are operated by Budapesti Közlekedési Központ, or **BKK**. Timetables, transport maps and more can be obtained from the BKK website.

BKK
W bkk.hu/en

Tickets

BKK runs an information centre at the airport where you can buy single tickets and longer-term travelcards. You can also buy them at self-service machines at metro stations, newsagents, and major bus and tram stops. Single tickets can be purchased from the driver on buses and trams, but cost an extra Ft150 and you will need the exact amount in cash. Single tickets need to be validated onboard buses, trolleybuses and trams, and at the entrance to metro stations.

Metro

Budapest has four metro lines, most easily distinguished by their colours: yellow (M1), red (M2), blue (M3) and green (M4). Three lines (M1, M2 and M3) intersect at Deák Ferenc tér station, while the M4 line intersects with the M2 at Keleti pályaudvar and with the M3 at Kálvin tér. Services run from 4:30am until 11:30pm.

Tram

There are more than 30 tram lines in Budapest, serving almost every part of the city except the hilly parts of Buda. Services start from about 4:30am, and run regularly until 11pm or midnight, depending on the route. Night trams operate only on line 6, every 10–15 minutes. BKK tickets and passes are valid along the line.

Bus and Trolleybus

Daytime bus services run from about 4:30am to 11:30pm, with departures on most routes every 10–20 minutes. Night buses operate across the city every 15–60 minutes. Departure times and destinations are displayed at each stop. Trolleybus routes run only in Pest.

Boats

Budapest has three public boat lines, the D-11, D-12 and D-14. In general, boats operate every 30–60 minutes between 6:30am and 8:30pm; however, timetables are seasonal. Passes and travelcards are valid during the week, but you need a special ticket at weekends or if you do not have a pass or a travelcard.

Taxi

Taxi ranks are located throughout the city and taxis can also be hailed on the street. To avoid inflated fares book from your hotel or by phone. **City Taxi** and Főtaxi are reliable options. Ridesharing services such as Uber are banned.

Citytaxi
W citytaxi.hu

Driving

This is the least convenient method of getting around Budapest. There are few places to park, traffic can be busy during the week and one-way systems can be tricky to navigate. If you do decide to drive, then a wide variety of car-hire firms, such as Hertz and Avis, can be found at the airport.

Cycling

Cycling in Budapest is often difficult. Cyclists have to be very careful of tram rails and the uneven surfaces of some roads. However, the main roads are usually open to cyclists and the opening of more cycle routes in the city has helped make cycling more popular.

Bikebase hire out bikes and there is also a public bike-sharing scheme called **MOL Bubi**.

Bikebase
W bikebase.hu

MOL Bubi
W molbubi.hu

Walking

Budapest is a great city for exploring on foot. Váci Street and Vörösmarty Square are car-free, as are many of the streets around the Royal Palace.

PRACTICAL INFORMATION

A little local know-how goes a long way in Budapest. On these pages you can find all the essential advice and information you will need to make the most of your trip to this city.

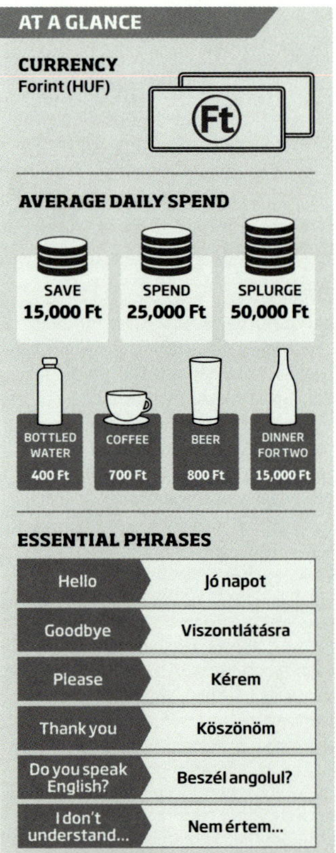

Passports and Visas

For entry requirements, including visas, consult your nearest Hungarian embassy or check the Hungarian foreign ministry's **Consular Services** website. Citizens of the UK, US, Canada, Australia and New Zealand do not need visas for stays of up to three months, but in future will have to apply in advance for the European Travel Information and Authorization System (ETIAS); rollout has continually been postponed so check website for details. Visitors from other countries may also require an ETIAS, so check before travelling. EU nationals do not need a visa or an ETIAS providing they have a valid passport.

Consular Services
W konzinfo.mfa.gov.hu/en

Government Advice

Now more than ever, it is important to consult both your and the Hungarian government's advice before travelling. The **UK Foreign and Commonwealth Office**, **US Department of State**, **Australian Department of Foreign Affairs and Trade** and **Hungarian Police** offer the latest information on security, health and local regulations.

Australian Department of Foreign Affairs and Trade
W smarttraveller.gov.au
Hungarian Police
W police.hu/en
UK Foreign and Commonwealth Office
W gov.uk/foreign-travel-advice
US Department of State
W travel.state.gov

Customs Information

You can find information on the laws relating to goods and currency taken in or out of Hungary on the **National Tax and Customs Administration** (NAV) website. If arriving from outside the EU, besides personal belongings you can bring the following items into the country – 40 cigarettes, four litres of wine, one litre of spirits and €300 worth of gifts. There are no limits on the import of goods from EU countries.

National Tax and Customs Administration
W nav.gov.hu/en

Insurance

We recommend taking out a comprehensive policy covering theft, loss, medical care, delays and cancellations. Read the small print carefully.

UK citizens are eligible for free emergency medical care using a valid EHIC (European Health Insurance card) or **GHIC** (UK Global Health Insurance Card). Visitors from outside the UK and EU must arrange for their own private medical insurance.

GHIC
W gov.uk/global-health-insurance-card

Vaccinations

No vaccinations are required for visitors to Hungary.

Money

Major credit and debit cards are accepted everywhere and contactless payments are increasingly common. Minimum amounts are often required for card transactions, so carry cash for smaller payments. ATMs *(bankautomata)* are available outside banks, as well as some shops. It is customary to tip waiters 10 per cent of the bill, hotel housekeeping Ft300 per day and concierge staff Ft300–500.

Travellers with Specific Requirements

Many of Budapest's attractions are located in areas with cobbled streets, narrow pavements, or steep slopes and steps, presenting difficulties for visitors with limited mobility; this is particularly true of sights in the Castle Hill area. Historic buildings often lack lifts or ramps, but larger hotels, restaurants and bars are now obliged to have accessible bedrooms and bathrooms. Newer trams and buses, and most metro stations, offer step-free access. **BKV** (Budapesti Közlekedési Zrt.) offers a door-to-door bus service.

The Hungarian Federation of Disabled Persons' Associations, more commonly known as **MEOSZ**, has a useful website with information on disabled access in Budapest – although currently only in Hungarian.

BKV
W bkv.hu/en/physically_challenged

MEOSZ
W meosz.hu

Language

Hungarian, or Magyar, is the official language in Hungary. English is widely spoken in Budapest by people working in the services industry.

ID

By law in Hungary, you need to carry your passport or national ID card with you at all times and present it to the police if asked to do so. You will be asked to present ID when checking in to accommodation, including private apartment rentals.

Opening Hours

Banks are generally open 9am–4pm on weekdays, though opening hours can vary significantly. Shops keep long hours from Monday to Saturday (often 10am–8pm), with malls staying open until 10pm. Many shops are also open on Sundays, but they might close earlier. You should find plenty of smaller shops selling basic necessities open 24 hours a day throughout the city. Most museums and other main attractions are open every day, although some are closed on Mondays.

Situations can change quickly and unexpectedly. Always check before visiting attractions and hospitality venues for up-to-date opening hours and booking requirements.

Personal Security

Budapest is generally a safe place but petty crime does take place. Pickpockets work busy public transport routes and known tourist areas – in particular in and around Váci Street. Rental vehicles can be targeted by thieves, so ensure no valuables are left inside the car. It is also a good idea not to take valuables to the thermal baths, as thieves may target lockers.

If you have anything stolen, report the crime as soon as possible at the nearest police station and take ID with you. Get a copy of the crime report to claim on your insurance. Contact your embassy or consulate if your passport is lost or stolen, or in the event of a serious crime or accident.

Hungary is a largely conservative society, with the result that LGBTQ+ communities are not always met with acceptance. In 2021, Hungary's government passed legislation barring people from changing their gender on official documents, and banning schools from discussing LGBTQ+ topics. Budapest itself, however, is more welcoming. The city has good LGBTQ+ friendly nightlife and hosts an annual, month-long Pride festival in June. If you do feel unsafe, the **Safe Space Alliance** pinpoints your nearest place of refuge. **Travel Gay**, meanwhile, has up-to-date recommendations on LGBTQ+ friendly venues and events.

Hungary's political situation is volatile, and demonstrations are common, especially around election time. These are usually held in Heroes' Square and should be avoided if possible.

Safe Space Alliance
W safespacealliance.com
Travel Gay
W travelgay.com

Health

Emergency medical care in Hungary is free for all UK and EU citizens, providing they have either an EHIC or a GHIC. You may have to pay after treatment and reclaim the money later.

Pharmacies are ubiquitous, well stocked and most are open seven days a week. If your nearest branch is closed, there should be a list displayed in the window of all the local chemists on 24-hour emergency duty.

Not all medical staff speak English. In an emergency, call an ambulance or

AT A GLANCE

EMERGENCY NUMBERS

GENERAL EMERGENCY	AMBULANCE
112	**104**

FIRE BRIGADE	POLICE
105	**107**

TIME ZONE

CET/CEST: Central European Summer Time runs from the last Sunday in March to the last Sunday in October.

TAP WATER

Unless stated otherwise, tap water in both Budapest and its surrounding areas is safe to drink.

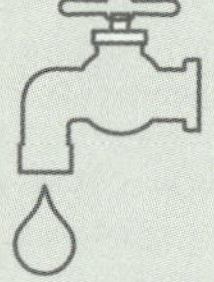

WEBSITES

Budapest Info
The city's official website has lots of useful information for tourists *(www.budapestinfo.hu)*.

Visit Hungary
The Hungarian Tourism Agency's official website and app is very good for planning excursions outside of Budapest *(www.visithungary.com)*.

We Love Budapest
The best independent source of events listings *(www.welovebudapest.com)*.

visit **Péterfy Kórház-Rendelőintézet**, the city's central 24-hour emergency room, near Keleti station. There are a number of private clinics with English-speaking staff and a higher standard of care, but these are expensive and neither EHIC or GHIC are accepted. The most central is **Medoc Klinika**.

Medoc Klinika
W medocklinika.hu
Péterfy Kórház-Rendelőintézet
W peterfykh.hu

Smoking, Alcohol and Drugs

Hungary has some of the EU's toughest anti-smoking legislation and smoking is banned in all indoor public spaces, including on public transport and in stations. Even when outside, smokers must be 5 m (16 ft) from a building entrance before lighting up. Cigarettes can only be purchased from branches of the national chain of tobacco shops *(Nemzeti Dohánybolt)*.

It is illegal to drive in Hungary after consuming any alcohol. If your blood alcohol level is above 0 per cent but under 0.08 per cent you will be fined; if it is 0.08 per cent or over, you will be subject to legal proceedings.

Hungary has a zero-tolerance anti-drugs policy, and possession of even the smallest amounts of illegal substances can land you with a large fine or a even prison sentence.

Responsible Tourism

The climate crisis is having a big impact on Hungary with an increasing number of heatwaves and droughts. Conserve water by taking quick showers. Visit lesser known baths to avoid over-crowding in the main tourist hotspots. Use public transport and deposit rubbish in bins, or take it with you.

Visiting Churches and Cathedrals

When visiting churches and religious sites, visitors should dress respectfully. Make sure you cover your torso, upper arms and knees.

Mobile Phones and Wi-Fi

Visitors with EU call plans can use their devices abroad without data roaming charges. Other visitors can buy a local SIM card in order to take advantage of local rates. Telenor, Vodafone and Telekom offer pre-paid SIM cards, sold at most newsstands, kiosks and mobile phone stores.

Budapest is well covered with Wi-Fi hotspots. The app **WiFi Map** lists most free Wi-Fi spots in the city.

WiFi Map
W wifimap.io

Postal Services

Hungarian mail is fast and reliable. Offices of Magyar Posta, the national mail service, usually open 7am–6pm. A postcard or standard letter weighing up to 20g costs Ft1020 to Europe or Ft1180 to other destinations.

Taxes and Refunds

The price of all goods in Hungary incl-udes a value-added tax of 27 per cent (ÁFA). With the exception of antiques and works of art, it is possible for non-EU residents to claim back this tax on anything costing more than Ft50,000. However, before buying expensive goods with the intention of reclaiming the VAT, it is advisable to consult the vendor about whether they have the necessary VAT-reclaim form. When leaving the country, present these papers with the receipt and your ID at customs to receive your refund.

Discount Cards

The Budapest Card entitles a visitor to use most city transport free of charge, and provides discounted or free entry to some museums. It also offers a discount on tickets to a number of selected spas, restaurants and many cultural events. Purchase it online via the **Budapest Info** website, at official tourist information centres or at the Liszt Ferenc International Airport.

Budapest Info
W budapestinfo.hu

PLACES TO STAY

From five-star palaces to budget hostels, restored heritage buildings to chic urban hotels, Budapest has a place to stay for every type of traveller. Whether you're looking for Danube views, in-house thermal spas or a locally run guesthouse, you'll find accomodation that suits your needs.

Budapest is well connected by public transport, so wherever you stay there's fun to be had exploring the local area. Staff are always happy to point you in the direction of the best attractions.

PRICE CATEGORIES

For a standard, double room per night (with breakfast if included), taxes and extra charges.

F: Under Ft30,000
FF: Ft30,000–60,000
FFF: Over Ft60,000

Castle District and North Buda

Kimpton Hotel Bem

B2 Bem József tér 3 ihg.com/kimptonhotels · FFF

The first Kimpton in Central and Eastern Europe, this luxury five-star hotel injects California cool into Budapest's historic core. Think bespoke cocktails at the rooftop bar, complimentary bikes for city exploration and a very popular evening wine hour.

Hilton Budapest

G2 Hess András tér 1-3 hilton.com · FFF

Imagine sleeping in a 13th-century Dominican monastery where monks once prayed, now transformed into a luxurious haven. Floor-to-ceiling windows frame perfect Parliament views while Gothic architecture blends seamlessly with contemporary design. It brings all the charm of historical Budapest while still feeling surprisingly current.

Hotel Clark

H3 Clark Ádám tér 1 hotelclarkbudapest.hu · FFF

Positioned exactly where the Chain Bridge lands on Buda, this sleek hotel offers views of one of the city's most-photographed sights. The rooftop bar is legendary for sunset sessions, and many of the minimalist rooms offer front-row seats to the Danube's daily comings and goings.

Pest-Buda Hotel

G2 Fortuna utca 3 pestbudahotel.com · FF

Budapest's oldest inn is now a design-forward retreat. The juxtaposition of exposed medieval walls with modern furnishings creates spaces that feel both timeless and totally now.

Baltazár Budapest

G1 Országház utca 31 baltazarbudapest.com · FF

A boutique gem where street art meets medieval charm. Each room tells its own story through original murals and vintage finds, while the location puts you steps from Mátyás Church – minus the tourist crowds. The courtyard breakfast area feels like a secret garden away from the bustling city.

Maison Bistro and Hotel

G2 Országház utca 17 maisonbudapest.hu · FF

This intimate hideaway in a restored townhouse feels more like a stylish friend's pied-à-terre than a hotel. It's an elegant place, with antique-filled rooms, high ceilings and parquet floors. Perfect for travellers who prefer charming character over corporate comfort.

Gellért and Tabán

Gold Hotel Budapest

H5 Hegyalja út 14 goldhotel.hu · FF

Genuine hospitality and insider tips come as standard at this hotel, a family-run treasure near leafy Tabán Park. With rooms that balance home comfort with modern style, it's great for anyone wanting to experience the city like a local.

Hotel Mediterran

N2 Budaörsi út 20a hotelmediterran.hu · FF

This sunny escape near Gellért Hill is punching above its weight with luxury extras like a sauna and jacuzzi. Here, Mediterranean vibes meet Magyar hospitality, and the comfortable and well-equipped rooms feature balconies overlooking quiet residential streets.

Kalmár Panzió

J6 Kelenhegyi út 7-9 kalmarpension.com · FF

This family-run guesthouse offers a cosy retreat with authentic Hungarian charm and a home-cooked breakfast served in the sunny courtyard garden. Its quiet location provides a peaceful respite while still being within easy reach of Budapest's vibrant attractions via nearby public transport.

Green Hill Apartments

J6 Kelenhegyi út 23a greenhillbudapest.hu · FF

Perched in the lush Buda hills, this accommodation combines modern design with panoramic city views that sparkle at night. Each self-catering unit has generous living space and amenities including full kitchens, washing machines and private balconies.

Hotel Charles

H5 Hegyalja út 23 charleshotel.hu · F

This hotel is a budget travellers' dream: affordable comfort not too far from the city centre. The breakfast room opens early for any eager sightseers, and the reception provides maps, restaurant recommendations and honest local advice about tourist traps to avoid.

Around Parliament

Prestige Hotel Budapest

K2 Vigyázó Ferenc utca 5 prestigehotelbudapest.com · FFF

Architecture buffs swoon at this belle-époque building, which manages to be sophisticated without being stuffy. Rooms feature marble bathrooms, Hungarian-made furniture and soundproofing that blocks the noise of the city. There's also a Michelin-starred kitchen on site – so don't be surprised to see the odd diplomat dining here (the hotel is mere steps from Parliament).

H2 Budapest

K2 Sas utca 24 h-hotels.com · FF

Situated in a meticulously restored heritage building, H2 Budapest seamlessly blends historic architecture with contemporary design elements. Its central location puts you right by the Danube Promenade and major tram lines connecting both sides of the city.

Four Seasons Hotel Gresham Palace

K3 Széchenyi István tér 5-6 fourseasons.com/budapest · FFF

Budapest's crown jewel of hospitality occupies an Art Nouveau masterpiece so stunning it's a tourist attraction itself. Wake to views of Chain Bridge through original stained-glass windows, surrounded by mosaics and ironwork that define the Hungarian Secession style. The in-house spa uses mineral-rich waters from Budapest's famous thermal springs.

Hotel President Budapest

L1 Hold utca 3-5 hotelpresident.hu · FF

At this hotel the rooftop terrace alone justifies a stay – 360-degree views put Parliament, Castle Hill and both bridges on full display from the terrace. Here in winter? Fear not. You can still enjoy the views from a heated "bubble" tent. Mod-cons offer substance to match the spectacular setting, with free Wi-Fi, comfortable beds and efficient air conditioning.

Ikonik Parlament

L1 Kálmán Imre utca 19 eurostarshotels.com • F

With its prime location offering unrivalled views of Parliament, this hotel delivers sophisticated urban living at a bargain price. The elegant rooms feature floor-to-ceiling windows that look out to the city's most iconic landmark, making every morning feel special.

Central Pest

Anantara New York Palace

D4 Erzsébet körút 9–11 anantara.com • FFF

Home to one of Europe's most beautiful cafés, the New York Café (which requires a reservation even for guests), this luxury hotel is all about Hungarian grandeur. The lobby is pure wow factor, all gilt, marble and frescoes, and the rooms are just as striking.

Matild Palace

L4 Váci utca 36 matildpalacebudapest.eu • FFF

This UNESCO-protected belle-époque palace, built in 1902, has been revived as Budapest's hottest luxury address. With its original details preserved and modern comforts added, like state-of-the-art lighting systems and a hip rooftop bar, this hotel has become the city's go-to spot for sundowners for good reason.

Dorothea Hotel

L4 Dorottya utca 2 dorotheahotelbudapest.com • FFF

Housed inside three historic buildings from the 19th and 20th centuries, this multi-award-winning hotel honours both history and modernity with innovative decor that blends contemporary style with local tradition. The restaurant is nestled in a scenic inner courtyard, complete with live trees and a unique vertical herb garden.

Stories Boutique Hotel

L3 Király utca 26 storiesbudapest.com • FF

This place is all about celebrating great art. Each suite channels a different creative theme, from vintage photography to avant-garde art installations, and the lobby even doubles as a gallery showcasing local artists.

Hotel Rum

L5 Királyi Pál utca 4 hotelrumbudapest.com • FF

Expect urban cool at this mid-range hotel. Its location puts you in the heart of Budapest's evolving creative scene and it features one of Pest's buzziest rooftop bars, ideal for those who come to the city for a good time. The lobby doubles as a hip coffee shop by day and stylish cocktail bar by night, too.

Hotel Zenit Budapest Palace

K4 Apáczai Csere János utca 7 budapest.zenithoteles.com • F

With contemporary rooms and a central location, this hotel ticks a lot of boxes. The best thing? It's affordable too. A great choice for those keeping it simple.

Around City Park

Mamaison Hotel Andrássy

E2 Munkácsy Mihály utca 5–7 mamaisonandrassy.com • FFF

If seeing the best of Budapest's cultural scene is top of your list, check out this Bauhaus-inspired place, right near Heroes' Square and Museum Mile. It's ideal for a longer visit, too, with rooms that feel residential rather than hotel-standard, thanks to kitchenettes, lounge areas and big bathrooms.

Mystery Hotel Budapest

D2 Podmaniczky utca 45 mysteryhotelbudapest.com • FFF

Gothic drama meets modern luxury at the Mystery Hotel, which leans into Hungary's folklore and legends. Expect secret passages, hidden libraries, and rooms featuring custom furniture inspired by fairy tales. There is also a secret garden spa located in a peacful inner courtyard, offering a range of treatments.

Mirage Medic Hotel

E2 Dózsa György út 88 miragemedic hotel.hu · FF

In need of some rest and relaxation after all your sight-seeing? You can't go wrong with this wellness-focused retreat. The health and relaxation philosophy extends beyond spa treatments to rooms designed for genuine restoration, such as a magnetic jade stone system in the core of each mattresses that is said to have therapeutic properties.

Lion's Garden Hotel

F3 Cházár András utca 4 lions-garden-hotel-budapest.com · FF

A peaceful retreat near City Park's attractions with unexpected perks like an indoor pool and private garden area. Proximity to Széchenyi Baths seals the deal for thermal spa enthusiasts, while families love the space and tranquility, as well as the hotel's babysitting services.

Benczúr Hotel

E2 Benczúr utca 35 hotelbenczur.hu · F

Located on a lovely tree-lined street, this hotel feels like a sanctuary. It offers remarkable value considering how near it is to major attractions, including Heroes' Square and the Museum of Fine Arts. A garden terrace and genuinely helpful staff, it's a rare find in this busy tourist area.

Alice Hotel

E2 Andrássy út 116 alicehotel.hu · F

An Andrássy Avenue address at a reasonable price is hard to come by, but that's exactly what you'll get with this smart villa conversion built in the late 1800s. Luxuries include a bed and breakfast service, cosy terrace and a stylish bar.

Greater Budapest

Ensana Thermal Margaret Island

B1 Margaret Island ensanahotels.com · FF

Have you ever stayed on an island? Now you can. Situated on beautiful Margaret Island, this quiet leisure hotel offers car-free surroundings and parkland views that create a serene resort atmosphere. Just minutes from downtown, and with direct access to therapeutic thermal springs, multiple pools and extensive spa facilities, this hotel is a destination in itself.

Verdi Aquincum Hotel Budapest

P1 Árpád fejedelem útja 94 verdihotels.com · FF

If the name didn't give it away, you'll find this modern hotel not far from ancient Roman ruins. With a spa that has healing waters, it offers authentic Hungarian wellness away from tourist crowds, and the pleasant rooms provide a peaceful retreat after relaxing spa treatments.

Tiliana Wellness and Spa

N1 Hárshegyi út 1-3 tiliana.hu · FF

This tranquil urban oasis, centred around its award-winning thermal spa complex, has multiple treatment pools, saunas and customized wellness rituals designed around Hungarian traditions. Rooms include wellness-focused amenities like aromatherapy diffusers, meditation cushions and healthy minibar options.

Fortuna Boat Hotel

C1 Szent István park, Pesti alsó rakpart fortunaboat.com · FF

Anchored permanently on the Danube, this floating boutique hotel offers a unique stay. Its gently rocking quarters allow for a surprisingly peaceful sleep and rooms feature nautical design elements and panoramic river views. The deck is a charming outdoor space for morning coffee or evening cocktails.

Morvai Panzio

Mogyoród, Gödöllői út 39 morvaipanzio.hu · F

This country guesthouse provides a peaceful rural escape just minutes from the excitement of the Hungaroring Formula 1 racetrack. Perfect for racing fans who want affordable accommodation with rooms that feature traditional décor and modern bathrooms.

INDEX

Page numbers in **bold** refer to main entries.

PHRASE BOOK

In an Emergency

Help!	**Segítség!**	*shegeetshayg!*
Stop!	**Stop!**	*shtop!*
Call a doctor	**Hívjon orvost!**	*heevyon orvosht!*
Call an ambulance	**Hívjon mentőt!**	*heevyon menturt*
Call the police	**Hívja a rendőrséget**	*heevya a ren-dur shayget*
Call the fire department	**Hívja a tűzoltókat!**	*heevya a tewzoltowkot!*
Where is the nearest telephone?	**Hol van a legközelebbi telefon?**	*hol von uh legkurze-lebbi telefon?*
Where is the nearest hospital?	**Hol van a legközelebbi kórház?**	*hol von a leg-kurze-lebbi koorhahz?*

Communications Essentials

Yes/No	**Igen/Nem**	*igen/nem*
Please (offering)	**Tessék**	*teshayk*
Please (asking)	**Kérem**	*kayrem*
Thank you	**Köszönöm**	*kurssurnurm*
No, thank you	**Köszönöm nem**	*kurssurnurm nem*
Excuse me, please	**Bocsánatot kérek**	*bochanutot kayrek*
Hello	**Jó napot**	*yow nopot*
Goodbye	**Viszontlátásra**	*vissont-latashruh*
What?	**Mi?**	*mi?*
When?	**Mikor?**	*mikor?*
Why?	**Miért?**	*miayrt?*
Where?	**Hol?**	*hol?*

Useful Phrases

How are you?	**Hogy van?**	*hod-yuh vun?*
Very well, thank you	**köszönöm nagyon jól**	*kurssurnurm nojjon yowl*
Pleased to meet you	**Örülök hogy megis-merhettem**	*ur-rewlurk hod-yuh megish-merhettem*
Where can I get…?	**Hol kaphatok …-t?**	*hol kuphutok …-t?*
How do you get to?	**Hogy lehet …-ba eljutni?**	*hod-yuh lehet …-buh el-yootni?*
Do you speak English?	**Beszél angolul?**	*bessayl ungolool?*
I can't speak Hungarian	**Nem beszélek magyarul**	*nem bessaylek mud-yarool*
I don't understand	**Nem értem**	*nem ayrtem*
Can you help me?	**Kérhetem a segítségét?**	*kayrhetem uh sheg-eechaygayt*
Please speak slowly	**Tessék lassabban beszélni**	*teshayk lushubbun bessaylni*
Sorry!	**Elnézést!**	*elnayzaysht!*

Useful Words

big	**nagy**	*noj*
small	**kicsi**	*kichi*
hot	**forró**	*forow*
cold	**hideg**	*hideg*
good	**jó**	*yow*
bad	**rossz**	*ross*
open	**nyitva**	*nyitva*
closed	**zárva**	*zarva*
left	**bal**	*bol*
right	**jobb**	*yob*
entrance	**bejárat**	*beh-yarut*
exit	**kijárat**	*ki-yarut*
toilet	**WC**	*vaytsay*
free/unoccupied	**szabad**	*sobbod*
free/no charge	**ingyen**	*injen*

Making a Telephone Call

Can I call abroad from here?	**Telefonálhatok innen külföldre?**	*telefonalhutok inen kewlfurldreh?*
Could I leave a message?	**Hagyhatnék egy üzenetet?**	*hud-yuhutnayk ed-yuh ewzenetet?*
Hold on	**Várjon!**	*vahr-yon!*

Shopping

How much is this?	**Ez mennyibe kerül?**	*ez menn-yibeh kerewl?*
Do you have…?	**Kapható önöknél…?**	*kuphutaw urnurknayl?*
Do you take credit cards?	**Elfogadják a hitelkártyákat?**	*elfogud-yak uh hitelkart-yakut?*
What time do you open/close?	**Hánykor nyitnak/zárnak?**	*Hahn kor nyitnak/zárnak?*
this one	**ez**	*ez*
expensive	**drága**	*drahga*
cheap	**olcsó**	*olchow*
size	**méret**	*mayret*
white	**fehér**	*feheer*
black	**fekete**	*feketeh*
red	**piros**	*pirosh*
yellow	**sárga**	*sharga*
green	**zöld**	*zurld*
blue	**kék**	*cake*
brown	**barna**	*borna*

Types of Shop

antiques dealer	**régiségkeres-kedő**	*ray-gee-shayg-kereshk-kedur*
bank	**bank**	*bonk*
bookshop	**könyvesbolt**	*kurn-yuveshbolt*
cake shop	**cukrászda**	*tsookrassduh*
chemist	**patika**	*putikuh*
department store	**áruház**	*aroo-haz*
florist	**virágüzlet**	*virag-ewzlet*
food store	**élelmiszerbolt**	*ail-ell-miss-er*
market	**piac**	*pi-uts*
newsagent	**újságos**	*oo-yushagosh*
post office	**postahivatal**	*poshta-hivatal*
shoe shop	**cipőbolt**	*tsipurbolt*
souvenir shop	**ajándékbolt**	*uy-yandaykbolt*
tobacconist	**trafik**	*trafik*
travel agent	**utazási iroda**	*ootuzashi iroduh*

Sightseeing

bus	**autóbusz**	*owtawbooss*
tram	**villamos**	*villumosh*
train	**vonat**	*vonut*
underground	**metró**	*metraw*
bus stop	**buszmegálló**	*booss megallaw*
art gallery	**képcsarnok**	*kayp-chornok*
palace	**palota**	*polola*
church	**templom**	*templom*
garden	**kert**	*kert*
library	**könyvtár**	*kurnvtar*
museum	**múzeum**	*moozayoom*
tourist information	**túristahivatal**	*toorishta-hivotol*
closed for public holiday	**ünnepnap zárva**	*ewn-nepnap zarva*

Staying in a Hotel

Have you any vacancies?	**Van kiadó szobájuk?**	*vun **ki**-udaw soba-yook?*
double room with double bed	**francia-ágyas szoba**	***front**sia-**ah**josh **sob**uh*
twin room	**kétágyas szoba**	***kaytad**-yush **sob**uh*
single room	**egyágyas szoba**	***ed-yad**-yush **sob**uh*
room with a bath/shower	**fürdőszobás/ zuhanyzós szoba**	***fewr**dur-**sob**ahsh/**zoo**-honzahsh soba*
porter	**portás**	***port**ahsh*
key	**kulcs**	*koolch*
I have a reservation	**Foglaltam egy szobát**	***fog**lultum ed-yuh **sob**at*

Eating Out

A table for… please	**Egy asztalt szeretnék… személyre**	*ed-yuh **us**stult **se**retnayk… **sem**ayreh*
I want to reserve a table	**Szeretnék egy asztalt foglalni**	***se**retnayk **ed**-yuh usstult **fog**lolni*
The bill please	**Kérem a számlát**	***kay**rem uh **sam**lat*
I am a vegetarian	**Vegetáriánus vagyok**	***veg**etariahnoosh **voj**ok*
I'd like…	**Szeretnék- egy…-t**	***se**ret nayk ed-yuh…-t*
waiter/ waitress	**pincér/ pincérnő**	***pints**ayr/ **pints**ayrnur*
menu	**étlap**	***ayt**lup*
wine list	**borlap**	***bohr**lup*
drinks menu	**itallap**	***it**allup*
glass	**pohár**	*pohar*
bottle	**üveg**	***ew**veg*
knife	**kés**	*kaysh*
fork	**villa**	*villuh*
spoon	**kanál**	***kun**al*
breakfast	**reggeli**	***reg**-geli*
lunch	**ebéd**	***eb**ayd*
dinner	**vacsora**	***voch**ora*
main courses	**főételek**	***fur**-aytelek*
starters	**előételek**	***el**ur-aytelek*
desserts	**desszertek**	*dess-air-tekh*
rare	**angolosan**	***ongo**loshan*
well done	**átsütve**	***aht**shewtveh*

Menu Decoder

ásványvíz	***ahsh**vahnveez*	mineral water
bárány	***bah**rahn*	lamb
bors	*borsh*	pepper
csirke	***cheer**keh*	chicken
csokoládé	***chok**olahday*	chocolate
cukor	***tsook**or*	sugar
ecet	***ets**et*	vinegar
fagylalt	***fod**yuhloot*	ice cream
fehérbor	***fe**heerbor*	white wine
fokhagyma	***fok**hodyuhma*	garlic
főtt	*furt*	boiled
gomba	***gom**ba*	mushrooms
gyümölcs	***dyew**murlch*	fruit
gyümölcslé	***dyew**murlch-lay*	fruit juice
hagyma	***hoj**ma*	onions
hal	*hol*	fish
hús	*hoosh*	meat
kávé	***kav**ay*	coffee
kenyér	***ken**-yeer*	bread
krumpli	***kroom**pli*	potatoes
kolbász	***kol**bahss*	sausage
leves	*levesh*	soup
marha	***mar**ha*	beef
mustár	***moosh**tahr*	mustard
paradicsom	***por**odichom*	tomatoes
párolt	***pah**rolt*	steamed
rizs	*rizh*	rice
bifsztek	***bif**stek*	steak
roston	***rosh**ton*	grilled
sajt	*shoyt*	cheese
saláta	***shol**ahta*	salad
sertéshús	***sher**taysh-hoosh*	pork
só	*shaw*	salt
sonka	***shon**ka*	ham
sör	*shur*	beer
sült	*shewlt*	fried/roasted
sült burgonya	*shewlt **boor**gonya*	chips
sütemény	***shew**temayn-yuh*	cake, pastry
tea	***tay**-uh*	tea
tej	*tay*	milk
tejszín	***tay**sseen*	cream
tengeri hal	***tenge**ri hol*	sea fish
tojás	***toy**ahsh*	egg
vörösbor	***vur**-rurshbor*	red wine
zsemle	***zhem**leh*	roll
zsemlegom-bóc	***zhem**leh**gom**-bowts*	dumplings

Numbers

0	**nulla**	***nool**luh*
1	**egy**	***ed**-yuh*
2	**kettő, két**	***ket**tur, kayt*
3	**három**	***har**om*
4	**négy**	***nayd**-yuh*
5	**öt**	*urt*
6	**hat**	*hut*
7	**hét**	*hayt*
8	**nyolc**	***n-yolts***
9	**kilenc**	***kil**ents*
10	**tíz**	*teez*
11	**tizenegy**	***tiz**ened-yuh*
12	**tizenkettő**	***tiz**enkettur*
13	**tizenhárom**	***tiz**enharom*
14	**tizennégy**	***tiz**en-nayd-yuh*
15	**tizenöt**	***tiz**enurt*
16	**tizenhat**	***tiz**enhut*
17	**tizenhét**	***tiz**enhayt*
18	**tizennyolc**	***tiz**enn-yolts*
19	**tizenkilenc**	***tiz**enkilents*
20	**húsz**	*hooss*
30	**harminc**	***hur**mints*
40	**negyven**	***ned**-yuven*
50	**ötven**	***urt**ven*
60	**hatvan**	***hut**vun*
70	**hetven**	***het**ven*
80	**nyolcvan**	***n-yolts**vun*
90	**kilencven**	***kil**entsven*
100	**száz**	*saz*
1,000	**ezer**	***ez**er*
10,000	**tízezer**	***teez**ezer*
1,000,000	**millió**	***mil**liaw*

Time

one minute	**egy perc**	***ed**-yuh perts*
hour	**óra**	***aw**ruh*
half an hour	**félóra**	***fayla**wruh*
Sunday	**vasárnap**	***vush**arnup*
Monday	**hétfő**	***hayt**fur*
Tuesday	**kedd**	*kedd*
Wednesday	**szerda**	*serduh*
Thursday	**csütörtök**	***chew**turturk*
Friday	**péntek**	***payn**tek*
Saturday	**szombat**	***som**but*

ACKNOWLEDGMENTS

This edition updated by

Contributors Craig Turp
Senior Editor Kiron Gill
Senior Designers Katie Cavanagh, Stuti Tiwari
Project Editor Lucy Sara-Kelly
Project Art Editor Bineet Kaur
Editors Eleanora Reeves, Catrina Conway
Proofreader Ben Ffrancon Dowds
Indexer Helen Peters
Picture Research Deputy Manager Virien Chopra
Senior Picture Researcher Nishwan Rasool
Assistant Picture Research Administrator Manpreet Kaur
Publishing Assistant Simona Velikova
Jacket Designers Bineet Kaur, Katie Cavanagh
Jacket Picture Researcher Diana Jarvis
Project Cartographer Ashif
Senior Cartographer James Macdonald
Cartography Manager Suresh Kumar
Pre-Production Coordinator Tanveer Zaidi
Pre-Production Designer Rohit Rojal
Pre-Production Image Coordinator Jagtar Singh
Pre-Production Image Editor Mohd Rizwan
Pre-Production Manager Balwant Singh
Pre-Production Image Manager Pankaj Sharma
Senior Production Controller Kariss Ainsworth
Deputy Managing Editor Dharini Ganesh
Managing Editor Beverly Smart
Managing Art Editor Gemma Doyle
Senior Managing Art Editor Priyanka Thakur
Editorial Director Hollie Teague
Art Director Maxine Pedliham
Publishing Director Georgina Dee

The publisher would like to thank the following for their kind permission to reproduce their photographs:

Key: a-above; b-below/bottom; c-center; f-far; l-left; r-right; t-top

Adobe Stock: Alfredo 26–27t; Haider Azim 16cla; Danita Delimont 11; Csák István 69t; Yury Kirillov 85; Geza Kurka 13clb, 17, 106.

Alamy Stock Photo: Naoki Morita / AFLO SPORT / Nippon News 10bl; ART Collection 9cr; Art Collection 3 10tl; Zoltán Csipke 48, 56, 67, 76; Ian Dagnall 14; Jim Zuckerman / Jaynes Gallery / DanitaDelimont.com 25; Rob Tilley / DanitaDelimont.com 40–41b; eFesenko 29t, 39bl; funkyfood London - Paul Williams 105; Eddie Gerald 22crb; John Green 15br; Gardel Bertrand / Hemis.fr 22bl, 94, 100; Hauser Patrice / Hemis.fr 95; Mattes René / Hemis.fr 49b; INTERFOTO / Fine Arts 93; John Kellerman 19, 27b, 73t, 81; Keith Levit 50b; Hercules Milas 28, 35t; Peter Moulton 15cb; Omar Marques / Pacific Press 88; Paolo Paradiso 60t; Mo Peerbacus 41tl, 53; piemags 10cl; PJPHOTO 13cl; Simon Reddy 61; The Picture Art Collection 10br; Viennaslide 87; Chris Howes / Wild Places Photography 69b, 103b; Zoonar / Ruslan Gilmanshin 75.

Arany Kaviár Étterem: 77.

AWL Images: Nadia Isakova 82; Ben Pipe 12cra; Ken Scicluna 109.

The Big Fish: Barnabas Imre 101.

Bridgeman Images: 9tl, © Archives Charmet 8.

Budai Gesztenys: 107.

Castan Group: 83.

Depositphotos Inc: Kiyechka 16br; Vera_ Petrunina 80.

Dreamstime.com: Anton Aleksenko 64–65b; Anilah 44; Baloncici 29b; Evgeniya Biriukova 59, 91; Jerome Cid 65t; Ioan Florin Cnejevici 45; Shchipkova Elena 97b; Evgeniy Fesenko 22cb; Kirk Fisher 12crb, 49t; Ricardo Furtado 13cl (8); Zoltan Gabor 38, 73b; Izabela 23 54–55b; Sergii Kolesnyk 79b; Legacy1995 22br, 92; Mitzobs 21cla, 97t; Rosemarie Mosteller 37t; Pedro2009 16cr; Petr Pohudka 52; Oleksandr Prykhodko 13cla; Rosshelen 55t; Tatiana Savvateeva 57; Alla Simacheva 58; Skovalsky 9tr, 104; Tartalia 39cb; Vividaphoto 20cl, 62–63t; Wirestock 47; Noppasin Wongchum 1; Uri Yerochov 39br; Zeytun Images 103t.

Four Seasons Hotels and Resorts - Gresham Palace: 89.

Getty Images: Hulton Archive / Stringer 9br; Moment / Alexander Spatari 6–7; Moment / Istvan Kadar Photography 23; Moment / Karl Hendon 5; Moment / kolderal 71; Moment /

lupengyu 12cr; Moment / zpagistock 15bl; The Image Bank / Sylvain Sonnet 16tc, 21c; The Image Bank Unreleased / Sylvain Sonnet 20bl.

Getty Images / iStock: E+ / Guven Ozdemir 15t; Fabiomichelecapelli 98–99; Eloi_Omella 86; Salvador-Aznar 13bl.

House of Music Hungary: György Palkó 30-31t, 31b

Hungarian National Museum: 42b.

Memories of Hungary: 63b.

Museum of Fine Arts Budapest: Gyula Benczr, The Recapture of Buda Castle, 1896 35b; Jzsef Rippl-Rnai, The Manor House at Krtyvelyes, 1907 / Berényi Zsuzsa 36.

Shutterstock.com: Andocs 66; Ungvari Attila 32–33b; csikiphoto 60b; DanielCz 79t; EQRoy 37b; Davor Flam 13tl; Arsenie Krasnevsky 42t; mehdi33300 12br; MikeDotta 50–51t; Pfeiffer 33t; V_E 74.

Cover images:

Front and Spine: **Getty Images:** Moment / Eric Yang; *Back:* **Alamy Stock Photo:** Rob Tilley / DanitaDelimont.com tl, Chris Howes / Wild Places Photography tr; **Dreamstime.com:** Zoltan Gabor cl.

Sheet Map:

Getty Images: Moment / Eric Yang.

A NOTE FROM DK

The rate at which the world is changing is constantly keeping the DK travel team on our toes. While we've worked hard to ensure that this edition of Budapest is accurate and up-to-date, we know that opening hours alter, standards shift, prices fluctuate, places close and new ones pop up in their stead. So, if you notice we've got something wrong or left something out, we want to hear about it. Please get in touch at travelguides@dk.com

Within each Top 10 list in this book, no hierarchy of quality or popularity is implied. All 10 are, in the editor's opinion, of roughly equal merit.

First edition 2006

Published in Great Britain by Dorling Kindersley Limited, DK, 20 Vauxhall Bridge Road, London SW1V 2SA

The authorised representative in the EEA is Dorling Kindersley Verlag GmbH. Arnulfstr. 124, 80636 Munich, Germany

Published in the United States by DK Publishing, 1745 Broadway, 20th Floor, New York, NY 10019, USA

26 27 28 29 10 9 8 7 6 5 4 3 2 1

A CIP catalog record for this book is available from the British Library.

A catalog record for this book is available from the Library of Congress.

ISSN: 1479-344X
ISBN: 978 0 2417 8330 6

Printed and bound in China

www.dk.com

This book was made with Forest Stewardship Council™ certified paper – one small step in DK's commitment to a sustainable future.
Learn more at **www.dk.com/uk/information/sustainability**